FENCING MANUAL: POINT AND COUNTERPOINT

Fencing Manual: Point and Counterpoint

Traité d'Escrime: Pointe et Contre-Pointe

Romuald Brunet

translated by Chris Slee

Fencing Manual: Point and Counterpoint
Copyright ©2024 Chris Slee (translator)

ISBN: 978-0-6452538-4-9 (Print)

Traite d'Escrime: Pointe et Contre-Pointe, Romuald Brunet. The original text is from a facsimile of the 1884 edition. It is asserted this book is in the public domain.

Created at LongEdge Press, first edition.

*To the LongEdge Fencing crew who bought
me the original. This is for you.*

Contents

Introduction

Point and Counterpoint provides one of the best outlines available of the developing French classical tradition in that it covers both foil, as the foundation of all fencing, and sabre, as an extension. It does not include épée, for reasons explained below, which clearly signals that this fencing style, regardless of the weapon used, is *conventional*.

For some fencing masters during this period, form is more important than merely hitting your opponent. Brunet certainly numbered himself among this group. The debate between "practical" and "conventional" swordsmanship marked the thinking of the post-Revolution, post-Napoleon fencing world, as did finding ways to manage the explosive growth of the sport after the Franco-Prussian War of 1870.

About the text itself, as always, Brunet is an absolute joy for the translator. His language is clean and precise, following the best models of the logical writing style which the period aspired to produce. Where the fencing term in the original is still applicable to the modern sport, the term has been translated into the modern English equivalent. Where the term in Brunet's text either carries a different meaning to the modern term or is no longer used in the modern game, it has been left in the original. Where editorial choices have been made about how to translate a phrase from French to English, the original phrase has been footnoted so that the reader may perform their own translation.

Romuald Brunet

Jules Auguste Romuald Brunet was born in 1844 to Jean Louis Brunet, a merchant or retailer from the Languedoc, and Julie Louise Boucherie. He married Mathilde Leuba on 9 May 1868 and had two sons, Raymond Jules, who became an "agricultural engineer", and

Gaston Louis, who was a lawyer at the Court of Appeals in Paris. His date of death is unknown but is suspected to have been between the World Wars. The exact location of his life before and during his military career is not known but we know that he maintained two houses in Paris, one at 37 rue Saint-Petersbourg and another, presumably from his wife's family, at 19 rue Clapeyron. This latter is also given as his Parisien address later in his life. He also bought a wine making estate just outside of Bordeaux.

He volunteered for military service in 1870 as a *sous-officier* (non-commissioned officer) of cavalry, probably in the 13e Regiment de Chasseurs à Cheval since he writes in retirement about this unit so often. Whether he enlisted before or after the declaration of war with Prussia and whether he personally saw combat in that conflict is not known. After an apprenticeship in this role for a dozen years, promotion came quickly with him being made a lieutenant of *chasseurs* (light cavalry) in 1883 and captain in 1888. In 1900 and 1904, he was promoted to *chef d'escadrons* (company or battalion commander) and *d'état major* (chief of regimental administration) in the 18e Corps, the territorial reserve in and around Bordeaux, where he lived at that time.

We are told that the fencing masters who taught him included, chiefly, Lozès for foil and Vigeant for sabre, and he was also taught by the Gamoty clan, father and son, both well known for their military service. He is recognised as one of the most active members of the Military Circle in Paris, a club of active duty and former soldiers, who met to maintain their fencing skills, and organised many fencing competitions and fêtes. He was also very active in the fencing scene in the Bordeaux, being named in Hoke's 1905 who's who of fencers of the region.

In 1894, Brunet purchases part of a wine making estate, Pont de Langon, south west of Bordeaux from Modesto Lorenzo de Valle e Iznaga, Count of Lersundi, for 131,000 Fr. Modesto Lorenzo, himself a former military commander for Spain and serving in its colonial territories in the Americas, and Brunet shared fencing and the army as a common background. Brunet wrote a weighty book describing the development and current state of the Spanish army, simply titled *L'Armée Espagnole*.

It is at Pont de Langon that Brunet reinvented himself. No longer the man of war, he became a man of the arts, writing extensively on military and fencing matters as well as composing a vast amount of music, which we still have today thanks to widespread printing and publishing of the sheet music. His repertoire includes fantasies, marches, mazurkas, and polkas.

The Pont de Langon property produced close to 70 tons of red wine and 5 tons of white wine each year, winning silver medals in 1895 and 1897 at the *Concours général agricole de Paris*. The sons, Raymond and Gaston, each inherited half the property when they married in 1903 and 1905, although we are unsure who married first. Wine production on the estate suffered a decline starting in 1908 and legal troubles afflicted the family which were not settled until the estate was sold in 1939. Wine production on the estate did not make a come back to these levels until the 1960s.

One of the more interesting aspects of Brunet's life is the military and civilian distinctions he was awarded. He was inducted into the *Legion d'honneur* twice, first as *chevalier* on 28 December 1889, and then as *officier* on 9 August 1904. He was also recognised as an *officier d'Académie*.[1] These awards are perhaps not surprising. More puzzling are his induction into two civilian orders.

Brunet was inducted as *officier du Nichan-Iftikhar*, a French colonial order specifically tied to Tunisia, which the French invaded in 1881, although participating in this campaign or the colonial administration does not seem to be a requirement and there is no record of him serving overseas. The second, *chevalier d'Isabelle la Catholique*, may be less surprising given his close friendship with Modesto Lorenzo. This order is awarded by the Foreign Ministry of Spain to Spanish nationals and foreigners for services for improving the nation's foreign relations.

A Century of Fencing Controversy

This introduction does not have the space to allow for these topics to be treated with the depth they deserve. My aim in the following paragraphs is to provide an embarrassingly brief overview of the social situation in which Brunet is writing and the audience he is writing for. Hopefully, these signposts will intrigue readers sufficiently to dive down these rabbit holes for themselves.

I've not mentioned here the social upheaval in the aftermath of the Franco-Prussian War of 1870 and subsequent year of occupation because Brunet has enough to say on this subject himself. The seething, simmering anger of *Revanchisme* is well known and I cannot do justice to it in the space allowed here.

---

[1] We assume this refers to the *Académie d'escrime de Paris*. See below.

Foil versus Épée

The Revolution at the end of the previous century saw the dissolution of all the ancient guilds, including the Corporation of the Masters of Arms of Paris which licensed those who taught fencing in the city and maintained the traditions accumulated during the Corporation's lifetime. This severed fencing's ties to its pre-Revolutionary past and created a vacuum into which new traditions could emerge and develop.

The new traditions were birthed by the wars of Napoleon and the subsequent social strife of the first half of the new century. In particular, the military officers and other ranks captured by the British and Allied forces before Waterloo were condemned to an existence in the prison hulks, often damaged and captured French vessels, moored in the English and Bristol Channels. To pass the time, they fenced with either their sidearms or facsimiles, and from this arose a new philosophy of fencing: *qui touche a raison*.[2] The new philosophy was attached to the épée, the civilian version of the sidearm those captured officers were accustomed to handling.

The masters of foil were, of course, outraged and fought to quash this upstart discipline and to protect their own livelihoods and remembered traditions. The foilist philosophy was summarised in the phrase, *à toucher et à ne pas recevoir*.[3] By Brunet's time, these philosophies were seen as separate, distinct, and entirely incompatible with each other.

To cater for an ever more wealthy clientele, fencing with the foil became increasingly sophisticated, intellectual and abstract. Foil was now largely divorced from its martial origins and was a game to be played in the clubs of the wealthy urban classes.

At the same time, the progress of fencing with the épée, particularly with the resurrection of the long discarded practice of duelling, saw it become nothing more than making a slight wound on an extended target, such as the opponent's sword arm. Épee-ists referred to their practice as "practical fencing"[4] and dismissed foil fencing with the pejorative, "conventional fencing."[5]. Of course, the masters of foil shot back. Foil, they said, aims to kill by striking at the opponent's heart. Little wounds to the limbs are surely inappropriate for weighty questions such as a man's honour.

---

[2] whoever hits is correct
[3] to hit without being hit
[4] *l'escrime de pratique*
[5] *l'escrime de convention*

This schism, between form and outcome, is alive and well in modern HEMA one hundred and fifty years later. *Plus ça change* ....

The (Re-)Introduction of Sabre to France

The nineteenth century saw the reliance on cavalry as a battlefield tool fade and for all practical purposes disappear from military doctrine. Cavalry retained its role as scouts, a means of communication and providing perimeter security, but the idea of the shock of a heavy cavalry charge to destroy an enemy's cohesiveness was gone. With it went the use of the sabre.

In the second half of the century, however, a new form of sabre was introduced into France by Italian fencing masters moving there to establish fencing schools. One reason for this migration of sword teachers from Italy was that there was simply too many of them to be sustained in that market. The demonstrations given by Italian sabre masters, such as Luigi Barbasetti and Antonio Conte, so fascinated the French fencing world that Italian masters found a ready supply of students to build and sustain their careers for decades. Another reason for the migration is the revival of duelling in France.

Duels in France were traditionally fought using the épée and to a lesser extent, the foil, both thrusting weapons, or weapons using the *pointe*. Duels elsewhere in Europe, most notably Italy, were contested with sabres, but sabres which were much lighter than their military forebears of previous decades. These sabres were civilian rather than military weapons.

The French fencing masters, whether part of the épée or foil tradition, denigrated this style of fencing which relied on the blade edge rather than the point and referred to it as *escrime contre-pointe*, "fencing not with the point." They could not even give sabre fencing its own name but needed to define it by what it was not.

However, the popularity of sabre fencing was undeniable and, gradually, the practice became not only accepted but encouraged. This form of sabre fencing was even introduced into the curriculum of the *École Normale* at Joinville-le-Pont. The sabre practice in France at this period owes very little to the traditions of the Napoleonic charge of the *cuirassiers* or relentless forward march of the infantry attack column. For this, we need to read the manuals of Bertrand (1801), Valville (1817) and Ivanowsky (1834). It was the light, Italian duelling sabre which was epitomised in the army *Fencing Manual* of 1877 rather than the heavy cavalry sabre of the past.

Military Teaching Methods

From the fabled beginning of time, fencing was taught one-on-one, fencing master to a single student – even in the army. But the Imperial decree of December 1869, which made the teaching of fencing in the army both obligatory for all enlisted personnel and free of charge, overturned this tradition and created a problem. How to deal with not having sufficient fencing masters to provide this service? Especially since it was well known that the low rates of pay for military fencing masters discouraged the better candidates from taking up the role.

The civilian world provided the army with a potential solution. Beginning with the *loi Guizot* (Guizot's Law) in 1830, all towns with more than 500 population had to provide a school for the boys of the town. During the century, further laws provided that the education delivered be obligatory, free of charge and secular. Out of this situation developed the idea for and several method of group learning, or education *en masse*, which the army now applied to training their fencing masters.

The idea of teaching *l'escrime simultanée*[6] did not originate with, but was definitely popularised by, Bertrand Lozès' in his *Théorie d'escrime simultanée*, appearing in 1862. This concept is very familiar to fencing practitioners today but was shocking to the fencing establishment of the day. Lozès called for all the students to be assembled into a number of ranks, lines of students awaiting instruction. The master calls out the actions to be performed and the students follow the master by the numbers. This is exactly how group gymnastics, the other contemporary physical education craze, was performed. When fencing was introduced at the *École normale* at Joinville, it was as an addition to the gymnastic curriculum. So, it made sense that fencing was taught in the same manner.

It cannot be said that opinions were divided on the utility of the methodology. Fencing masters were almost universally against the practice and it was rapidly dropped as the preferred pedagogy at Joinville in favour of more traditional methods. The tried and true won out over the novelty of progress. Henri Hébrard de Villeneuve, who founded the one of the organisations which would in time become the modern French Fencing Federation and himself an Olympic medallist, commented that training in this way "was a type of gymnastics very agreeable to watch, but no serious fencer could be trained with this method."

---

[6]The literal translation as "simultaneous fencing" does not feel quite correct.

A Military or Civilian Career?

The Corporation of the Masters of Arms of Paris was abolished, along with all the other guilds and corporations of the *Ancien Regime*, in 1791 by decree of the Revolutionary Council. The Corporation was founded under the auspices of King Charles IX in 1567 and for more than two hundred and thirty years was the guardian of the traditions of fencing in France. After its abolition, there was no one and no organisation to keep these traditions alive and they slowly withered away, each fencing master developed his own way of doing things.

The physical culture movement, which had firmly taken root in the public mind by the middle of the nineteenth century, latched onto fencing as a uniquely French sport which must be developed, in part because it was opposed to those particularly English sports such as cricket and the various codes of football. The call for more fencing masters increased and was given explosive acceleration by the humiliation of the defeat of 1870. Before this time, in the entire country there was less than fifty fencing masters. By 1890, there was more than a hundred in Paris alone.

With no centralised body to certify fencing masters or warrant their skill at teaching the discipline, how could the general public assure themselves they were getting the quality of training they demanded and were paying for? Providing some assurance were the ancient and still well respected fencing dynasties in which sons followed fathers in learning the family trade of teaching fencing. These included the families Daressy, Mérignac, Vigeant, Prevost, Ruzé, among others. These names are well known to those interested in the history of French fencing.

The only organisation which certified fencing masters was the army's *École normale* at Joinville, which introduced fencing into its curriculum in 1867. It was here that those recruits selected to become fencing masters in the army completed their education in how to teach the discipline and were awarded a *brevet* certifying them as fully qualified to teach the army's fencing curriculum. This is precisely the role fulfilled by the Corporation in pre-Revolutionary times.

The army now had another problem to deal with. Soldiers were gaining their fencing master qualification at Joinville and leaving the army as soon as they could to make more money in the civilian world. In response, the army lifted prohibition against teaching civilians for those military fencing masters posted to regional France. Here, they may, on application and approval, provide lessons to interested members of the communities in which they were posted. In Paris, however, these measures were too late to stop the exodus from the army and rapid increase in fencing salles run by ex-army fencing masters.

While there were many fencing and sporting organisations created during this period, such as the *Société d'encouragement de l'escrime*, they declined to certify fencing masters. The credential imbalance between civilian and (ex-) military fencing masters was not corrected until 1897, when the *Académie d'armes de Paris* was founded by the leading civilian fencing masters and began certifying fencing masters in the city.

References

Dantarribe, C. *L'Histoire de Cateau Cousins: l'histoire réunie de deux châteaux viticole. Étude historique.* INRA Centre Bordeaux-Aquitaine. 2019.

Daressy, H. *Archives des Maitres d'Armes de Paris.* Quantin. Paris. 1888. (Available in translation as *The Archives of the Masters of Arms of Paris* from LongEdge Press.)

Grisier, A. *Les Armes et le duel.* Dentu. Paris. 1864.

Hébrard de Villeneuve, H. in Lahure, A. (ed.) *Propos d'épée 1882-1894.* Paris. 1894.

Hoke, W.S. *Bordeaux Fleuret. Editions de la Vie Bordelaise.* Bordeaux. 1905.

Joseph-Renaud, J. *L'Escrime.* Pierre Lafitte. Paris. 1911.

Lauvernay, L. *La Belle Époque de l'Escrime: naissance d'un sport.* Jas (42110). Ensiludium. 2024.

Lozès, B. *Théorie d'escrime simultanée. Librairie militaire dumaine.* 1862.

Ministère de la Guerre. *Manual d'escrime. Imprimerie nationale.* Paris. 1877. (Available in translation as *Fencing Manual 1877* from LongEdge Press.)

Tavernier, A. *Amateurs et salles d'armes de Paris*, C. Marpon et E. Flammarion, 1886.

Vigeant, A. *Duels de maîtres d'armes.* Motteroz. Paris. 1884.

FENCING MANUAL: POINT AND COUNTERPOINT

EUGÈNE CHAPERON 88

PREFACE

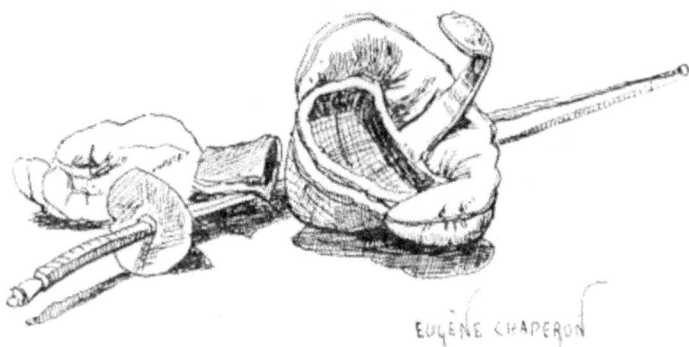

EUGÈNE CHAPERON

Fencing is a truly French art and a promoter of health.

In publishing this Fencing Manual today, our sole aim is to contribute to the great work of the military education of French youth, which we believe is the only way to ensure the independence and greatness of our country. It is, indeed, about developing strong, capable generations. We aim to create men, soldiers, who combine physical strength and agility with mental calmness and courage. Children must be given a taste for physical exercise, which will develop their limbs and ensure their health, at the same time as the habit of discipline and obedience, the basis of all military training, qualities essential to all those who want one day contribute to the defence of their country. Fencing is the most complete exercise and the best suited to making young people supple and vigorous. It is also the one where reflection and intelligence play the greatest role. It is therefore important to popularise such a useful science: this is the aim of this Manual. May our efforts be crowned with success! To our thinking, physical exercises, and in particular fencing, are a reasoned preparation for war and,

5

if it is unfortunately too true that "might takes precedence over right," perhaps it will be good to remember that instruction takes precedence over force itself.

R. BRUNET.

EUGENE CHAPERUN

INTRODUCTION

Fencing, taught according to the rational method and simplified as much as possible, must be included, like gymnastics, in the physical education of young people.

If we refer to the famous historian Herodotus, the ancient Greeks attached great importance to all bodily exercises. This author notes that these same Greeks owed their victories and the preservation[7] of their independence to the strength and agility of their warriors, almost always, however, inferior in number to their enemies. The Romans cultivated, even more than the Greeks, the science of arms and the learning of discipline; so they became the premier soldiers in the world.

An example taken at random from Herodotus will show us how much the ancients valued physical vigour.

Cleisthenes, tyrant of Sicyone,[8] a rich and powerful man, had a daughter named Agariste, and was not a little troubled in choosing a husband for her. He invited the suitors to compete in various exercises, so that he could distinguish between them the strongest or the most skilful. It is reported that Hippoclides seemed to be the probable winner of the fights and games when at a meal, this Athenian, instead of starting with the warlike dance, the "Pyrrhic", performed the effeminate dances of Ionia. — Cleisthenes, irritated, immediately cried out: "Son of Tisander, your dance undoes your marriage!" Indeed, he later gave his daughter to Megacles, son of Alcmaeon, an illustrious warrior among all the young Greeks.

According to history, Nero was the first to use a thrusting sword against his adversaries, gladiators armed with tin foils.[9] Marcus Aurelius, more humane, had the gladiators given iron foils, which allowed

---

[7] *le salut*

[8] An ancient Greek city state situated in the north of the Peloponnese near the Gulf of Corinth.

[9] *de fleurets d'étain*

them to effectively defend their lives. — At the height of Roman power, sword fighting always featured in gymnastic games, spectacles attended by immense crowds from all the countries of the Empire. The building of the Baths contained fencing rooms, and the citizens of Rome held this exercise in great honour, because they rightly considered that handling a sword well is a true science.

Later, in the Middle Ages, the shape and lightness of the sword made it the offensive weapon par excellence. Its use became universal in Italy, France, Germany and Austria. It was then that foil fencing was born, a sort of sword with a square blade, ending in a button protected with leather.

Our fencing school dates from the Italian wars in the sixteenth century, but it has not adopted, in assaults and duels, the Italian custom of the coat wrapped around the left arm as a shield, of the dagger held in the left hand as an auxiliary weapon. The French School wanted people to take off their clothes and measure themselves bare-chested. It chooses a linear game, composed of attacks and parries, engagements and disengagements, free strikes and feints, ripostes and counter-ripostes. From this definition, we can immediately conclude that the art of fencing consists of the principle of executing the aforementioned movements, in the composure and appropriateness of the fencer.

The use of the sabre passed from the East to Germany around the 5th century and remained there until the Crusades, around which time it became almost general.

The sabre has undergone various transformations: formerly, it had a curved blade with one edge which went all the way to the end, widening at an angle. Today, in almost all countries, it consists of a steel blade, called *bancal* or *latte*, depending on whether it is curved or straight, that is to say suitable for cutting and thrusting, or only suitable for thrusting. — As with the sword, composure, aptness and skill are necessary in *contre-pointe* fencing.

Man, by fencing, whether with sabre, sword, or foil, obtains muscles of steel and acquires robust health, scorns fatigue and gains that composure and assurance which double the strength. This exercise is the best of all from a physical and moral point of view. — The science of fencing is cultivated in large centres, but unfortunately is very neglected in less important localities. For some time now, however, its use is becoming widespread, and we see many people from outside the army frequenting the rooms, taking lessons there and making assaults there. We cannot encourage enough these meetings which are so useful in carrying out the program of our military education.

In France, the sword is the national weapon. We hope that fencing becomes more and more widespread, and is more and more practised. If this Manual can contribute even a little, as we dare to hope, we will truly believe that we have made a work of patriotism.

FENCING MANUAL

Basis of Instruction

The instruction is divided into two parts:

1. Fencing with sword or *pointe*;

2. Fencing with a sabre or *contre-pointe*.

These two parts each include seven articles.

Part One – Fencing with the Sword or with *Pointe*

Fencing, henceforth, is part of compulsory and free education. It is regulated in the daily schedule of work of French youth.

Article I

General principles and spirit in which this science must be taught.

The teacher, by adapting his teaching to the physical faculties as well as the intelligence of the student, and by being identified, I would even say, with his strength if he puts himself within his reach, makes the lesson truly attractive and fruitful.

It is through calm, patience and work that the instructor saves the student from unnecessary fatigue and useless lengths, the first condition for achieving a conclusive result, that is to say, for obtaining a correct position of the hand and the body, gradually accelerating movements to gain precision and speed, essential qualities of a complete fencer.

The intelligent and conscientious teacher himself maintains a classic position under arms, and thus serves as a model for his student, who is jealous to imitate him.

From the first lessons, he shows himself to be implacably severe in the application of the first principles, on which depends, as everyone knows, the future skill of a fencer who, otherwise, instead of having a sword and a timely precision, to be skilful and beautiful in the gym, would fall into the mediocrity of vulgar amateurs.

The master makes his observations in a clear and precise manner to allow the student to quickly grasp the correlation between attack and defence, and thus to regulate his game with composure when he

15

TABLEAU EXPLICATIF

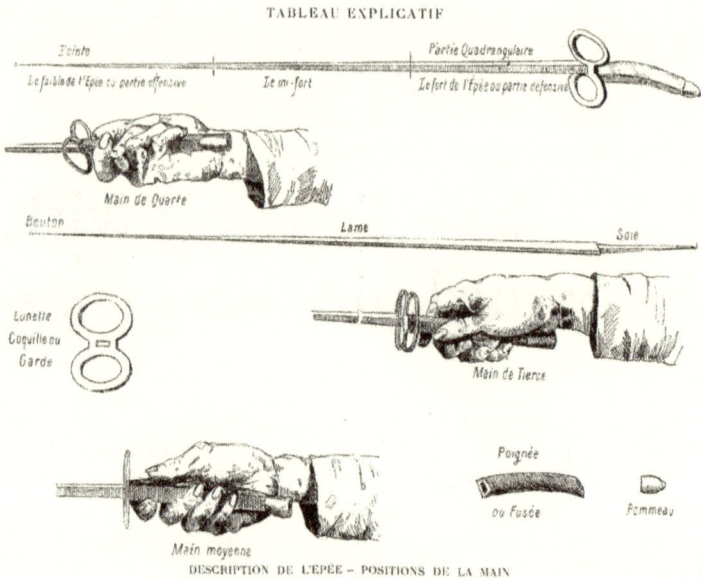

Explanatory Diagram

makes an attack.

The first condition for an exact fencer is to leave all self-esteem aside and to understand that the phases of any fencing assault consist of: throwing, getting up, parrying, riposting and counter-riposting, proceeding from the simple to the compound and by deceiving the parries. Fencing constitutes a conversation. In fact, the succession of blows delivered, ripostes and even counter-ripostes, constitutes in the language of fencing: a phrase.

It is therefore essential to grasp all the nuances and to understand the relevance[10] of the final movement of the opponent's as well as accuracy in the application of the principles, if one wants to become a practical fencer, a head fencer, a scientific fencer.

Article II

Description of the sword, movements, and definitions of the words used for attack and defence in fencing language.

---

[10] *de posséder l'à-propos*

(See Explanatory Diagram)

The salle sword, usually called foil, is divided into two parts: *the blade* and *mount*.

The *blade*, quadrangular and of steel, consists of three parts:

The *point* or *the weak*, *weak part* previous or *offensive part* garnished with a button covered with leather;

The *middle*, or *middle part*, or *medium strong*, in front of which are made *the engagements*;

The *heel* or *the strong*, *strong part* posterior or *defensive part*.

The *point* used to attack;

The *middle* to engage the blade;

The *strong* to parry.

The *blade* holds on to the mount *the tang* which is riveted *at the pommel*, the counterweight of the blade.

The *mount* includes three parts: *the guard*, with two iron lunettes trimmed with leather protect the thumb.

The *handle*, or spindle in ash or beech, covered with a leather wound by string or brass wire braids;

The *pommel*, small ball placed at the end of the handle.

Depending on the size, the foil takes from the longest and heaviest type, No. 5. — No. 4 and No. 5 are the most commonly used, either in ordinary work or in assaults. .

The length of the blade of n°4 up to the lunette is 0.84m; that of the handle of 0.165m. The length of the blade of n°5 up to the lunette is 0.88m; that of the handle of 0.175m. The weight of No. 4 is approximately 290 grams; that of n°5 is approximately 355 grams.

The best blades come from Saint-Étienne since the annexation of Alsace and Lorraine. In the past, Klingenthal provided us with a lot of them.

The assault or combat sword, buttoned or unbuttoned,[11] varies little in length as blade and handle with the salle sword, but it has a triangular blade and an iron guard in the shape of a shell with a concave surface, instead of the two glasses of the salle sword. Its weight is approximately 410 grams.

Sword in Hand

Take the sword in the whole hands, the thumb extended on the back of the handle up to the guard, the other four fingers closed underneath

---

[11] *mouchetée ou démouchetée*

without stiffness, the index finger used to hold the sword with the thumb, the other three fingers are only tightened for the parry.

When attacking and parrying, hold the sword firmly. In engagements, in disengagements, in *coulés*, in circular parries or in feints always have a light hand, that is to say the "touch",[12] to clearly feel the touch of the opponent's sword. A hard hand is never worth anything. The supple hand and the free wrist better meet the conditions of a fencer who holds his sword from tip to hilt according to the correct method and who seeks to prevent numbness of the muscles.

Principal Hand Positions

(See Explanatory Diagram)

The old demonstrations include three positions: *tierce, quarte, middle*.

Today, we also teach three positions: *sixte, quarte* and *middle*.

Let's talk about old positions:

With the hand in *tierce*, the nails are below, the back or convex surface of the hand above;

With the hand in *quarte*, the nails are above and the back or concave surface of the hand below;

With the hand in *middle*, the hand is between the two previous positions, i.e. 1/2 *tierce*, 1/2 *quarte*.

The new positions only differ from the old ones by the position of *sixte*, which is in short the corollary of that of *tierce*, but with a considerably less blade engagement.

To attack and riposte, you must therefore go through all these positions and their subdivisions.

We will give the complete nomenclature because, unlike several authors on the subject, I believe that it is good to teach the student, immediately, *all hand positions, and terms used in fencing and saluting under arms*.

The adversary facing opposite, the side of the heart is the side called the inside side. The opposite side is the side called the outside side.

First Position – *Prime*

The hand in *tierce*, at the height of the forehead, the thumb below, the elbow bent, the point lowered. Position: low inside.

---

[12] *doigté*

Second Position – *Seconde*

The hand in *tierce*, at the height of the breast. Position: low outside.

Third Position – *Tierce*

The hand at the height of the breast, the nails below, the point facing the opponent's eye, the arm shortened, Position: high outside.

Fourth Position – *Quarte*

The hand at breast level, the nails above, the point facing the opponent's eye. Position: high inside.

Fifth Position – *Quinte*

Hand low and in *tierce*, blade parallel to the ground. Position: high inside. .

Sixth Position – *Sixte*

The hand at the height of the breast and slightly in a *quarte* the point facing the eye of the adversary. Position: high outside.

Seventh Position (or Semicircle) Ellipse Described from Left to Right – *Septime*

The hand in a *quarte*, the wrist at the height of the chin, the arm open, the point at the height of the opponent's breast. Position: low inside.

Eighth Position (or Semicircle) Ellipse Described from Right to Left – *Octave*

The wrist at chin level, the arm open, the point at the height of the opponent's breast. Position: low outside.

Flexibility[13] or Preparatory Work

To perform well at arms, it is essential to have a flexible body which does not fear fatigue. For this, the teacher will have to prepare the students without the foil.

---

[13] *les assouplissements*

On command: *Left and right open files,* the student in the centre does not move and each student placed on the right and left makes a right or a left step, placing themselves two meters from the one in the centre.

The body straight, the head straight, the eyes fixed on the instructor, the flexibility exercises are carried out as commanded:

At the call: *Attention.* Or at the whistle: (SHORT.)

At the call: *Begin.* Or at the whistle: (SHORT, LONG.)

Until the indication of:

By voice: *Stop.* Or on the whistle: (LONG, SHORT).

The instructor, at the beginning, has the students break down the movements and mark the rhythm by announcing them with one, two, three, etc, following the movements. All movement can be preceded by the command:

By voice: *In position.* Or to the whistle: (SHORT)

The exercises are first performed at a moderate pace to reach all possible speed.

The flexibility exercises of the body and the flexions of the extremities are done slowly.

In the position with the arms in the air or vertically; arms forward or horizontally, fists closed, nails inward.

Bending the Upper Extremities or Deployment of the Arm and Forearm.

In the position of the unarmed soldier.

Horizontal Bending

Bend your arm, elbow back, fists forward.

Horizontal Extension

Vigorously extend your arm to its full length.

Horizontal Bending

Bring your arm back, elbow bent, fist forward.

Vertical Extension

Raise your arm in the air to its full length.

Horizontal Bending

Lower and bend your arm, elbow back, fist forward.

Lateral Extension

Straighten your arm to its full length along your thigh. These movements can be done with both arms.

Rotation of the Arm Backwards and Forwards

These movements mainly prepare for *contre-pointe* fencing. Despite this, we insist on their necessity as a preparation for the sword to supple the muscles.

With the arm outstretched (horizontal extension), have it describe an arc from bottom to top, grazing the thigh and raising the body on points of the feet.

Bending the Lower Extremities or Softening of the Legs

1. Bring your fists to your chest, join your feet, body forward, lower your body with your legs closed, your thighs against your calves forming an acute angle with your knees at the top, the weight of your body resting on your heels.

2. Get up slowly and squarely without wobbling.

Bending the Trunk Forwards and Backwards

1. Incline the body forward, describing an arc of a circle whose ground is the rope, the arms extended, the hamstrings stretched.

2. Get up slowly, bending backwards, lower back tightened, fists at hip height (horizontal bending of the arm), elbow back, legs slightly bent, heels slightly raised from the ground.

Bending the Lower and Upper Extremities Combined with Each Other.

1. Place the right foot 0.60m in front of the left foot, fists on the chest, bend the body forward, the front leg bending, the back leg straightening, the arm stretched horizontally or parallel to the ground.

2. Raise the body, place the fists on the chest, lean the body backwards, the front leg straight, the back leg bent, throw the fists vertically in the air, the gaze following the movement.

3. Bring your fists to your chest.

4. Return to the unarmed position, bring the right foot next to the left foot.

Alternate Thigh Flexing

With your fists on your hips, raise your right and left thighs successively so that they are horizontal at the pace of the quick step and oblique at that of the gymnastic step.

Flexing of the Thighs, Legs and Arms

1. Join your feet, bend your legs, bring your arms back, raise them vertically while raising your body as high as possible on tiptoe.

2. Fall back on your feet while bending your arms, place your hand laterally on the seam of the pants.

Jumps

1. In the position with the fists near the hips, with a firm foot, with feet together, in a free stance, the jumps are executed in width, in height and in depth or all combined.

2. With feet together, same movements.

3. In free position, that is to say when the jump is preceded by a run, the student, having arrived near the obstacle, shortens his step, strikes the ground with one or the other foot, to lift himself off, bringing his legs together which he bends, then falls to the ground with his feet together, bending, and straightens up gently.

In long jumps, the student throws his arms forward. In high and deep jumps, he throws them into the air. — The ground for the jumping should be firm. The ground for jumping down, softened.

Movements Without the Foil

1. In the position of the unarmed soldier, heels on the same line and close to each other, feet at right angles, knees straight, body plumb on the hips, make a half to the left, that is to say a half-quarter circle by pivoting on the left heel, and bringing the right foot next to the left, keep the head direct, the right arm extended and forward towards the ground, the hand closed, the left arm falling naturally, the hand open.

2. Bend the thighs, round the left arm at the height of the top of the head, the hand resting on the wrist, bring the right leg to about 0.60m from the left foot, the heels on the same line, the body withdrawn, the right arm half bent, the hand closed at the height of the breast.

3. Having the weight of the body on the left leg, quickly extend the right leg to its full length, the foot perpendicular to the knee, the left thigh forming a spring, the left arm falling naturally along the left thigh, at the moment when the right foot rests flat on the ground, the hand open and detached from the thigh, the body following the impulse and always in balance, the right arm extended and parallel to the ground.

4. Rise to the position of the second movement, bending the left thigh, the right foot 0.60m from the left, the left arm rounded, the right arm half bent, the hand at breast height.

5. Take the first position, bringing the right foot next to the left foot, the left arm falling naturally along the left thigh, the right arm extended forward towards the ground.

Stepping

In the position of the second movement, learn to step. Bring the right foot firmly forward, the body upright, the left foot following at a distance of 0.60m.

Withdraw

Bring the left foot squarely back, the body still upright. The right foot follows at a distance of 0.60m.

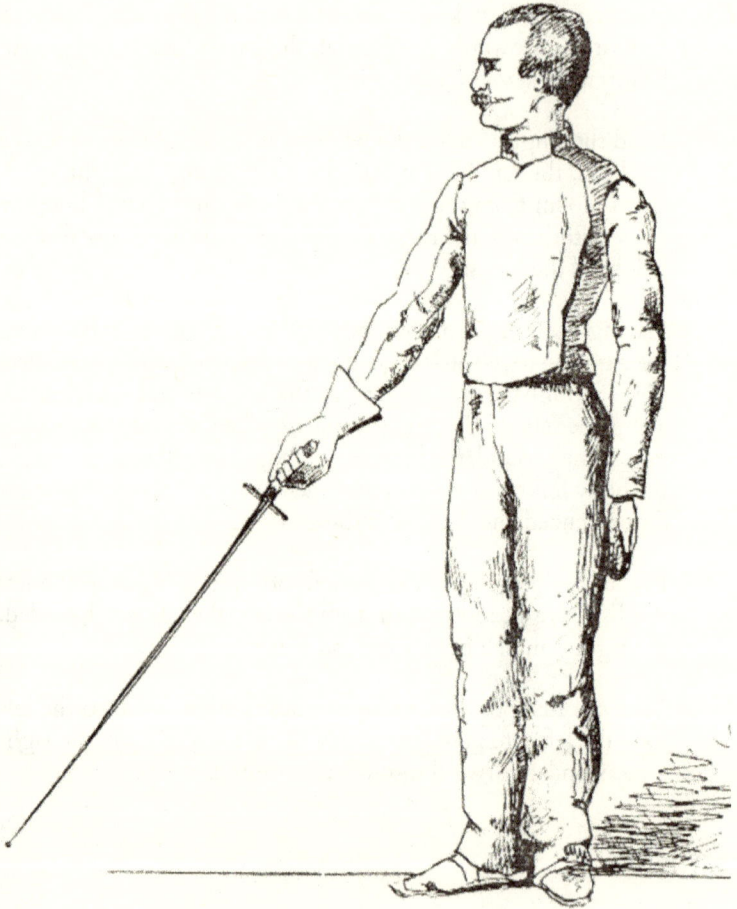

Deuxième mouvement pour se mettre en garde.
(Planche 1.)

Second movement to put oneself on guard (Plate 1)

Guard

Preliminary to attack, defence, riposte and counter-riposte.

(Position of the second movement.)

1° The body gathered together, the feet at right angles, the arm extended, the sword outstretched.

(First position of the movements without foil.)

With the point of the sword forming the apex of the angle of which the arm holding the sword is one side, and the line going to the feet the other side, raise the hand to eye level, the middle hand, the thumb above, the arm outstretched, the point in line with the arm.

2° Lower the sword, arm extended towards the ground, the tip 0.10m from the ground. (*Plate 1.*)

3° Gather up the sword parallel to the ground against the left thigh, the right hand in *tierce* (nails down), the left hand open and arched against the guard, the fingers resting on the blade.

4° Raise the sword above the head, bending and extending the arm, the blade resting flat on the fingers of the gracefully rounded left hand,

5° Separate the arms, the left rounded, the hand at the height of the head, the hand convex on the outside; the thumb detached, the arm bent at the height of the right breast, the elbow 0.15m from the body, the point of the sword at eye level. (*Plate 2.*)

6° Bend your legs, spread your knees, body level on your hips, right foot 0.60m from the left. (*Plates 3 and 4.*)

7° Lunge by extending the right foot, after having imperceptibly moved the hand ahead of it, the left leg supporting the weight of the body and forming a spring, the right knee vertical in relation to the foot, the left hand lying naturally on the left thigh. (*Plates 5 and 6.*)

Gathering

For the gathering: bring the right foot 0.60m from the left, the arm bent, the sword at the height of the right nipple, in the direction of the eyes, the left hand at the height of the gracefully rounded head.

The gathering is done forward and backward.

Appels

With the body upright, motionless, and the mind determined, strike the ground twice with the right foot. The *appels* are executed without preparation.

Deuxième mouvement pour se mettre en garde.

Second movement to put oneself on guard (Plate 2)

Suite du deuxième mouvement pour se mettre en garde.
[Planche 3.]

Continuation of the second movement (Plate 3)

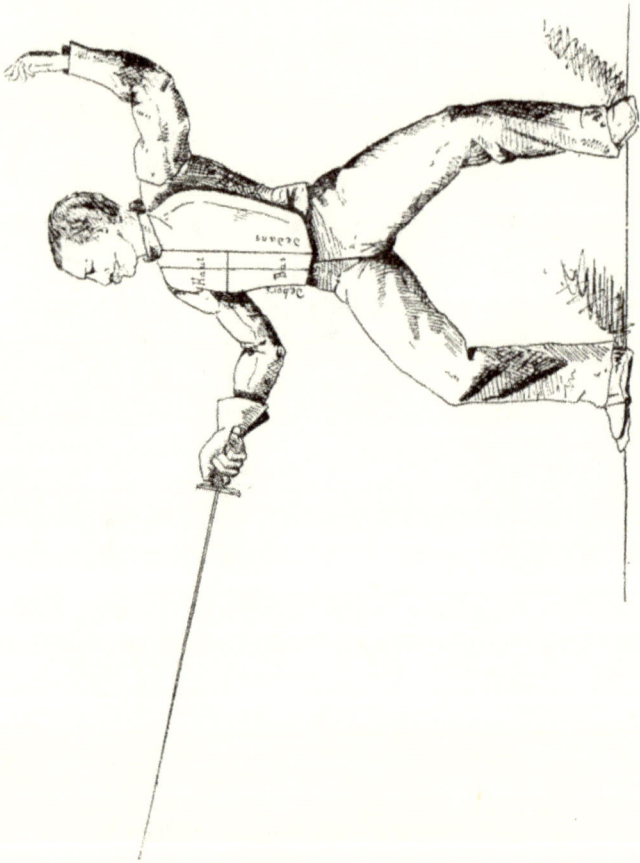

First movement of development (Plate 4)

Suite du deuxième mouvement pour le développement.

(Planche 5.)

Continuation of the second movement for development (Plate 5)

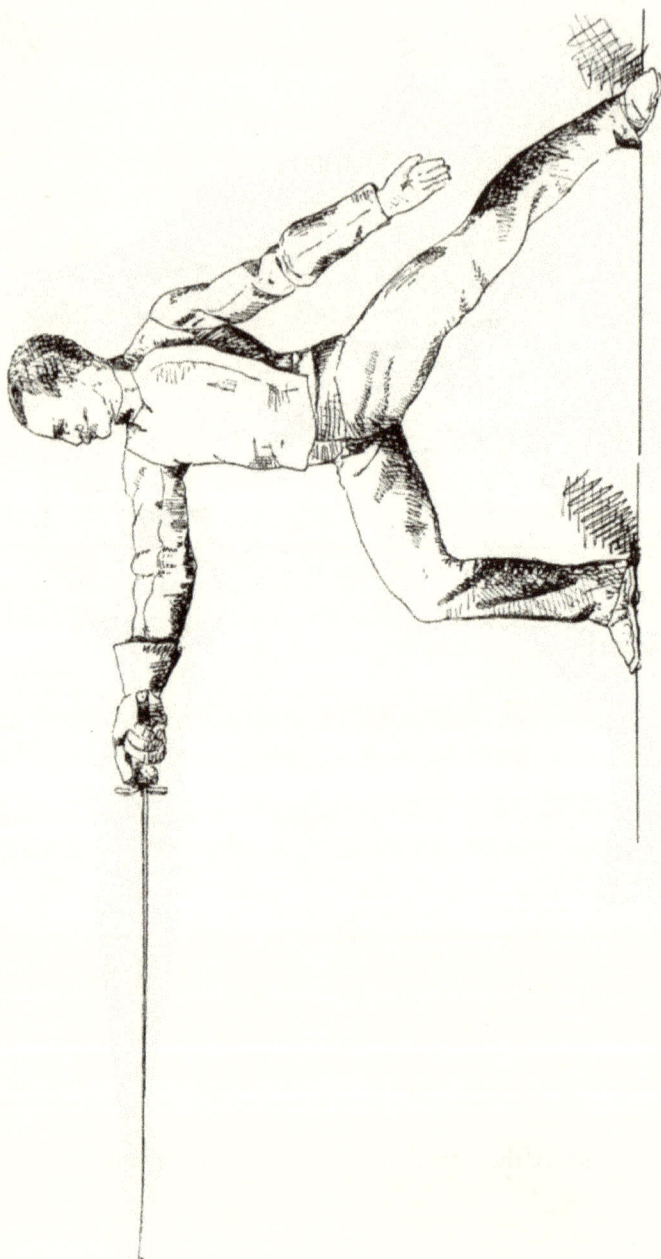

Deuxième mouvement du développement.
(Planche 6)

Second movement of development (Plate 6)

Stepping Forward

With the body straight, extend the right foot while bringing the left 0.60m from the right.

Stepping Backward

With the body straight, bring the left foot forward and place the right foot 0.60m from the left foot.

Arm Movements

In the guard position, take the guard position (nos. 5 and 6), always without jerking, by moving the wrist joint above which you must always see.

In the lunge position, take the position of guard no. 7, aiming vigorously at the target, effortlessly and frankly, the right arm extended to its full length, the left thigh springing and giving an impulse to the right leg whose knee must be perpendicular to the foot, the head straight, the eyes fixed on the point of the sword, put oneself back on guard and make sure by *appels*, if the body is well upright. — We can, in position en garde n°5 and 6, extend the arm without lunging, this is what we call extending the sword. We will have the opportunity to speak about it again in feints and other movements.

Simple Salute

At the position of the second movement for the guard, that is, at the position of the gathering.

1. Feet square and together, arm extended, sword stretched towards the ground, point 0.10m from the ground, arm half extended, elbow close to the body, guard 0.10m from the ground, thumb extended on the hilt, other four fingers together.

2. Extend the arm while lowering the blade, the hand in *quarte* near the right thigh, the nails above, hand concave.

Compound Salute or the Wall (6 beats.)

The salute of arms, called the wall, besides being very graceful when well done, gives suppleness to the body and makes the fencer more sure of himself. It even becomes imposing, if it is proudly established.

This salute is practised today only by masters, which is a great mistake in my opinion. The ordinary salute is preferred because of its simplicity.

The compound salute is made in six beats.[14]

1st beat:

1. The right hand in *tierce*;

2. Raise the left hand;

3. Bend the legs;

4. Move the right foot forward 0.60m from the left (guard position);

5. Gather backwards.

Say out loud to your opponent: *The honour is yours.*
This one must answer you: *In obedience.*

2nd beat:

For the one who said first: *The honour is yours* :

1° Lunge
2° Gather;

3° Salute; { 1° Salute to the left, head to the left, hand in *quarte*;
2° Salute to the right, head to the right, hand in *tierce*;
3° Gather.

4° Put yourself on guard. — Join the swords.

3rd beat:

1. At your disengagement, the opponent parries in *tierce*:

2. Put yourself on guard;

3. At your disengagement, the opponent parries in *quarte*;

4. Put yourself on guard;

5. One, two, gather forward, the opponent parries with *tierce*;

6. With the hand in *tierce*, raise the left arm;

7. Break off one step and keep guard;

---

[14]The original has *tempi*. However, this is better understood as musical beats or steps, rather than as *tempo* in the sense of fencing time.

8. Two *appels*;

9. Gather backwards.

4th beat:
  For the one who answered: *In obedience* : Like the 2nd beat.
5th beat:
  Like the 3rd beat.
6th beat:

1. With the hand in *tierce*, raise the left arm;

2. Withdraw

3. Two *appels*;

4. Salute as 3rd movement of 2nd beat, and gather forward;

5.   1. Raise the sword by bending the arm, the sword vertical and 0.10m from the shoulder, the nails turned towards the body;

      2. Lower the blade by extending the arm, the hand in *quarte* next to the right thigh.

Lines

The lines are divided into main lines or lines of engagement; into intermediate lines, into which one strikes, and into opposition lines, which one uses to cover oneself on the right and left, above and below.
  There are two main lines:

Main Lines (Facing the Opponent.)

1. Right or *tierce* line, or outside zone;

2. Left or *quarte* line, or inner zone.

Intermediate Lines

1. High line or *prime* line, or line above the wrist;

2. Low line or *seconde* line, or line below the wrist.

Let us also mention: the lines of opposition, which guarantee the straight strike, either by engaging the sword, or by parrying, or by riposting to the left and to the right, above and below, or by counter-riposting. In this movement, the wrist joint alone is involved, and, while throwing the opponent's sword away from the body, one must keep one's own in line to riposte freely.

The parry in opposition is made with the middle hand.

Engagements

To engage the blade is to make contact with the opponent's blade, passing underneath by the shortest line, the wrist to the left, the thumb above.

To cover oneself is to cross the sword, the hand on the right, the thumb above.

In both positions, the tip of the sword is at eye level.

Engaging and cover oneself include various variations:

1. Change of engagement or the counter to the previous engagement;

2. Double engagement or simultaneous engagements.

Fingering

In the guard position we talked about position of the hand and the action of the fingers. The thumb, index finger and third finger provide the sword strike. The other two are only used to grip the weapon in certain obligatory cases, such as oppositions.

Fingering is the finishing touch to the fencing design conceived by the fencer. A hard or tight hand and a soft or loose hand are both equally defective. To hold a sword well is a talent, and to hold it light and strong at the same time is not given to everyone.

Sword Strikes

Sword strikes are divided into simple strikes and compound strikes; the former involve only one movement, the latter several.

Single Strikes

1° Straight Strike

Extend your arm in the position you are in, if it is open, your hand raised and held to cover yourself, lunge freely, your left foot forming a spring, your body forward and upright.

2° Disengaging

Same movement as the change of engagement, but with one more phrase: the touch. To do this, pass the sword underneath, along the shortest line, quickly extend the arm, lunge and touch while keeping the wrist on the sword side to cover yourself.

3° Cutovers

1. Simple cutover or disengaging over the point. Raise the point of the sword, pass it as close as possible to that of the opponent, gaining the blade on him, and quickly extend to touch him;

2. Disengaging cutover or disengaging over the point, followed by a clearance under it. Raise the point of the sword, pass it as close as possible to that of the opponent, gaining the blade on him, the arm extended, releasing underneath to touch him.

Feeling, Tact and Intelligence in the Strikes.

This is pressing the opponent's sword from the point to make it come out of its line and strike more perfectly to hit him.

Froissement

To *froisser* the opposing sword, press the blade from one end to the other while sliding over it.[15]

Coulé

The *coulé* is a straight strike, not executed fully, that is to say without touching, and which is done by sliding along the sword.

---

[15] A form of thrust with opposition.

Beat

To strike a sharp blow to knock the opponent's sword out of line and thrust easily.

Binding

It is to be master of the opponent's sword, by pressing with the strong part of the sword, on the weak part of the opponent's sword to bring it to the low or high line, and vice versa.

The bind always requires an outstretched arm.

Whatever the engagement, take the half-circle parry, pressing the strong on the weak with the arm outstretched, lunge and touch while maintaining the opposite sword.

Dérobement

This movement is performed when the sword is passed from the high line to the low line, or vice versa.

After simple or compound strikes, disengage underneath, lunge and touch in the low line, raising the hand.

Remise

After the parry, on an absence or abandonment of the sword, touch with the straight strike without getting up, the sword well in line.

The *remise* is a matter of feeling.

Reprise

On the parry without a riposte, resume contact with the blade, without getting up and touching. .

Doubling

We call doubling repeating the same disengage twice, the first being a feint to lead the opponent to take the counter and to be able to freely work a second disengagement.

Redoubling

This move consists of two successive and immediate attacks.

Stop Strike

This is surprising your opponent in his step. Here, the glance and timeliness are everything.

Time Strikes

The time strike is taken on an attack by the opponent, an attack too wide where the foot went before the hand, or even on a feint which took the sword out of its line.

This strike thus surprises the opponent in his finish and closes the line. It constitutes a riposte and a parry.

Feint

A feint is the beginning of the execution of a strike that can end with a final move: a touch. Feints can be simple or successive. To feint is to strike in one line, with the intention of executing in another.— Each strike, in fencing, has its feint.

Parry

The parry is an opposition to the opponent's blade to throw it off its line. When you are master of your parry, you have a good chance of winning over your opponent. This quality is obtained through constant work and attention.

Counter or Variety of Parries.

The counter is a circular and tight parry which is taken in the line where the opponent's sword is presented, to gather it and chase it into the opposite line.

Of the Eight Parries

We said at the beginning of our work that there were eight hand positions or eight strikes. We can divide them as follows:

These eight strikes include eight parries and consist only of the straight strike combined with one or more disengages, depending on the opponent's game.

As for secret strikes, serious minds have already done them good and prompt justice for a long time.

HAUT

Sixte	*Quarte*
Tierce	*Quinte*

DEHORS ———————————————— DEDANS

Seconde	*Prime*
Octave	*Septime*

BAS

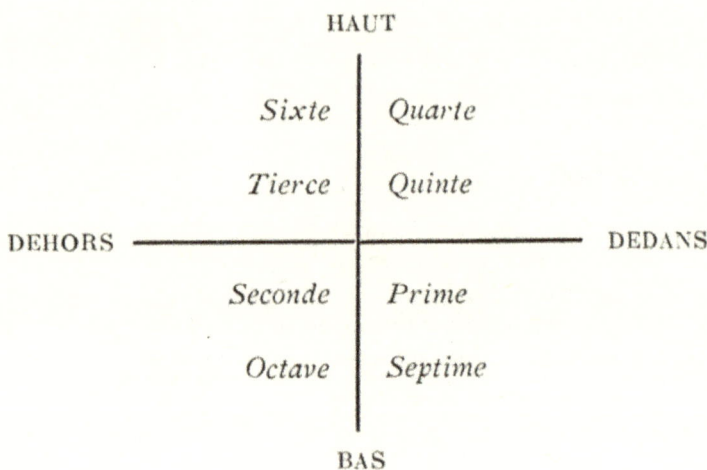

The Eight Parries

Each of the eight parries of *prime, seconde, tierce, quarte,* fifth, sixth, seventh and *octave* has its counter, a parry which is very successful when the adversary does not know how to deceive it.

According to the above table :

Two parries are executed high in the outside line: sixth and *tierce.*

Two parries are performed high in the inside line: *quarte* and *quinte.*

Two parries are performed low in the outside line: *seconde* and *octave.*

Two parries are performed low in the inside line: *prime* and *septime.*

Parry of First – *Prime* (*Plate* 7.)

Attacked on your left line, raise your elbow, extend your forearm so it is horizontal, with your hand in *tierce* at the level of your left eye. Your sword should threaten your opponent's lower line while their sword passes out of reach, close to your left chest. If you make contact, extend your arm slightly rotated so that your hand ends up in *quarte.*

To take the counter in *prime,* gently sweep the tip of your sword over the opposing sword, bringing it back to its previous position.

Attaque et parade de prime.

(Planche 7.)

Attack and Parry of *Prime* (Plate 7)

Parry of Second – *Seconde* (*Plate 8.*)

Attacked in the low line, turn the hand in *tierce*, slightly from left to right, the arm horizontal, the sword likewise, your sword threatening the opponent's chest and his passing out of reach, near the lower abdomen. If you touch, extend the arm, the hand slightly forced in *tierce*.

To take the counter of *seconde*, pass your sword over the opposing sword, bringing it back to the previous position.

Parry of Third – *Tierce* (*Plate 9.*)

Attacked in the right line, have the hand in *tierce*, the nails above,[16] the point of the sword at the height of the opponent's right eye by a play of the wrist joint, the point of your sword a little above the opponent's head, his at the height of your mouth. If you touch, extend your arm, the hand in *quarte*.

To take the counter of *tierce*, when attacked on the left line, confidently pass your sword over the opposing sword to bring it back to its original position.

Parry of Fourth – *Quarte* (*Plate 10.*)

Attacked in the left line, bring the hand to the left in *quarte*, using only a movement of the wrist, the point of your sword at the height of the opponent's left eye. If you touch, extend the arm placed naturally.

To take the counter of *quarte*, attacked in the right line, finely pass your sword over the opponent's sword to bring it back to its previous position.

Parry of Fifth – *Quinte* (*Plate 11.*)

Attacked in the left line, forearm lowered, middle hand at navel height, threatening the opponent's left breast, his sword out of reach of your lower abdomen on the left. If you touch, raise your arm in an ellipse, hand in *quarte*.

To take the parry of fifth, attacked in the straight line, pass your sword over the opposing sword to bring it back to its original position.

---

[16]Surely, this is a typo and should be "the nails below"; *en dessous* rather than *en dessus*.

Attaque et parade de seconde.

(Planche 8.)

Attack and parry of second (Plate 8)

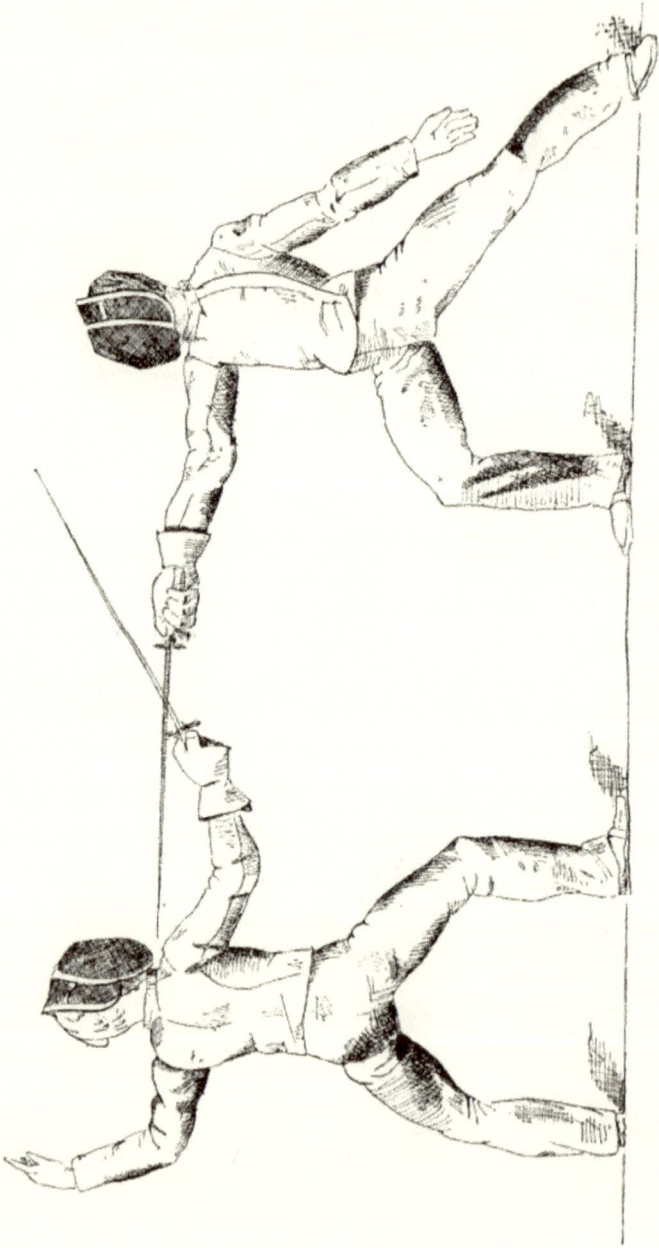

Attaque et parade de tierce

(Planche 9.)

Attack and parry of *tierce* (Plate 9)

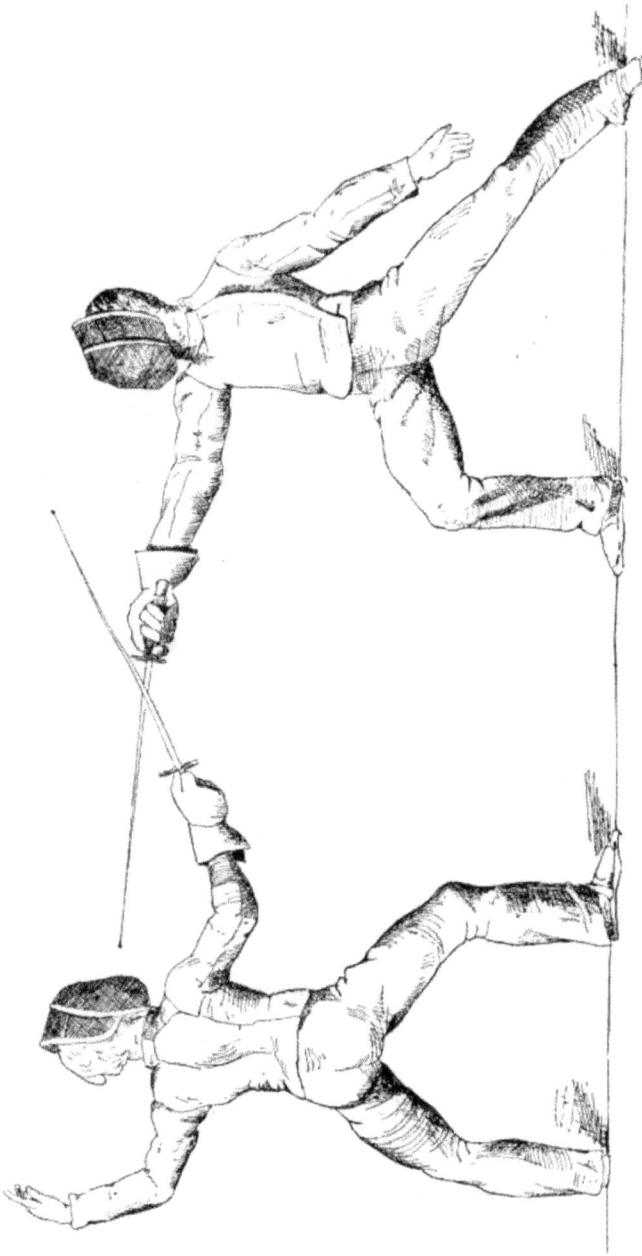

Attaque et parade de quarte.

(Planche 10.)

Attack and parry of *quarte* (Plate 10)

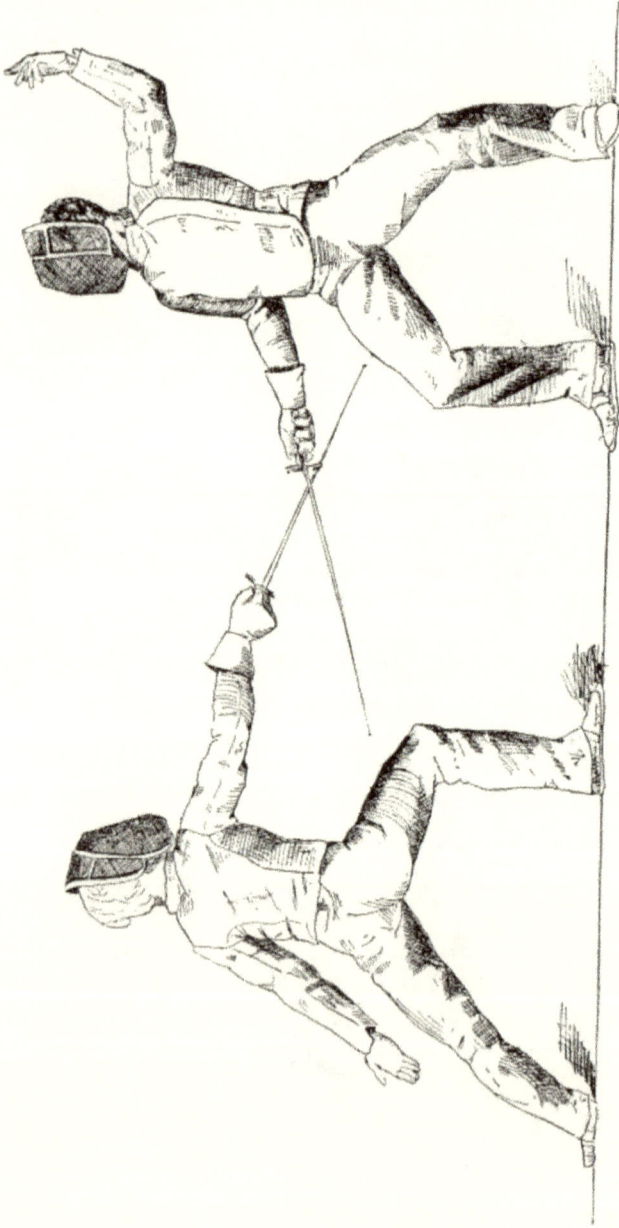

Attaque et parade de quinte.
(Planche 11.)

Attack and parry of the fifth (Plate 11)

Parry of Sixth – *Sixte* (*Plate 12.*)

Attacked in the straight line, bring the middle hand to the right, making a movement of the wrist, the tip of the sword at the height of the right eye.

To take the counter of sixth, attacked in the left line, pass the sword under the opponent's sword, and bring it back to its original position.

Parry of Seventh – *Septime* (*Plate 13.*)

Threatened in the low line, place the sword below the opponent's wrist, the hand at the same height in *quarte*, going from right to left. If you make contact, extend your arm fully.

Parry of Eight – *Octave* (*Plate 14.*)

Attacked in the low line, the hand at the same height turned in *quarte*, placing the sword under the opposing wrist.

To take the counter of *octave*, attacked in the low line, pass your sword over that of your opponent and bring it back to its original position.

Summary of the eight parries.

If we review the eight parries, we find that for *prime* and *seconde*, the first parry is taken in the lower inside line, while the second parry is executed in the lower outside line. For *tierce* and *quarte*, one is taken on the opponent's weapon, the other within the opponent's weapon. For fifth and sixth, one is executed within the opponent's weapon, the other on the opponent's weapon. For seventh and *octave*, one is performed in the lower inside line, the other in the lower outside line.

Ripostes

We have successively studied the engagements, and the parries. We still have to talk about the ripostes.

The most beautiful is that of the *tac-au-tac*, or touching the sword and the chest, that is to say, that which immediately follows the parry.

The others are done after a specific moment, following the opponent's phrase.

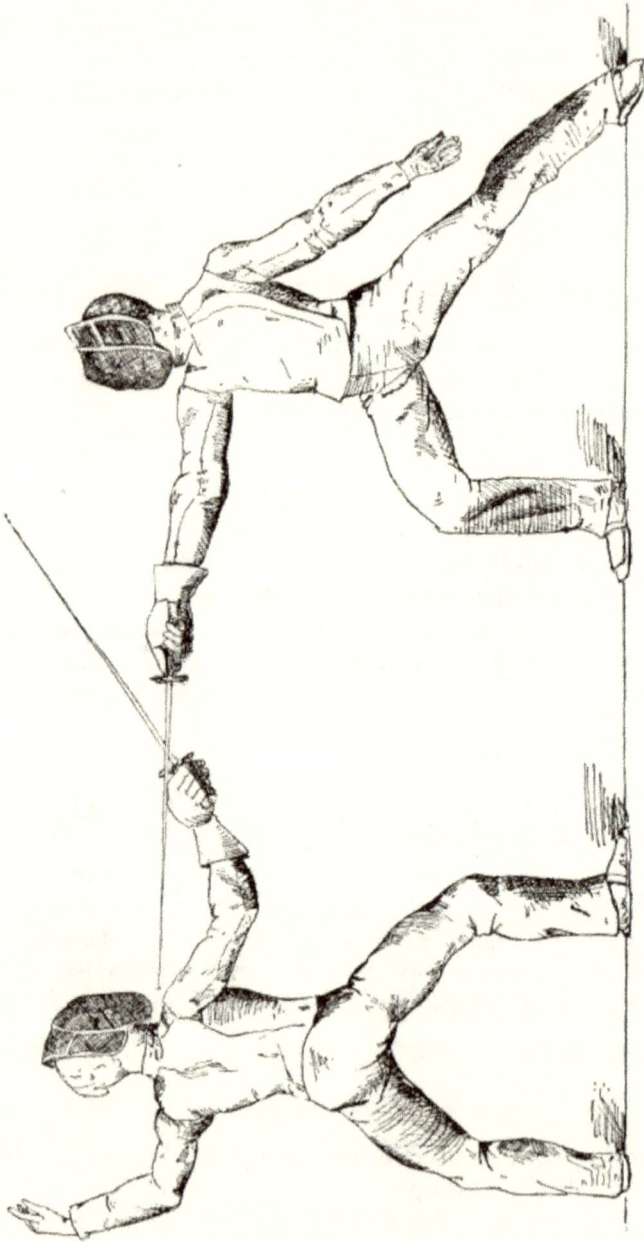

Attaque et parade de sixte.
(Planche 12.)

Attack and parry of sixth (Plate 12)

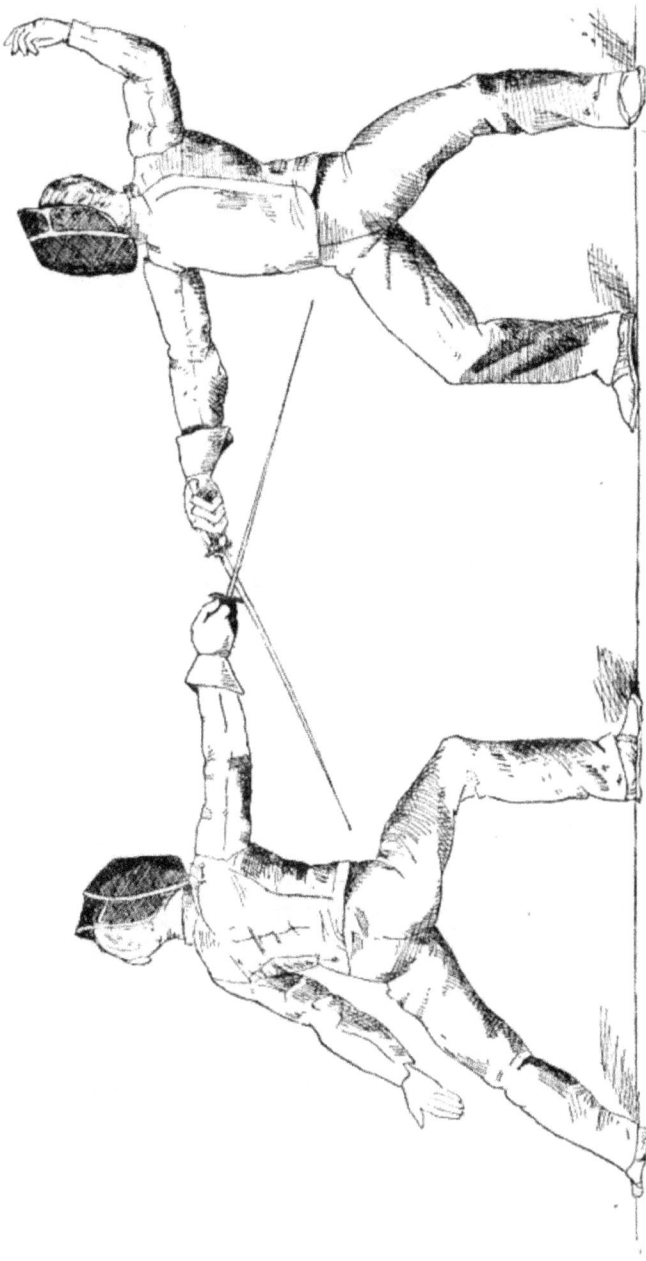

Attaque et parade de septime.

(Planche 13.)

Attack and parry of seventh (Plate 13)

Attaque et parade d'octave.
Planche 14.

Attack and parry of *octave* (Plate 14)

Article III

Statement of the general rules to be observed following the most rational method.

To become skilled in arms, one must start slowly, without rushing. Excessive speed in the first lessons can lead to bad habits, which may be impossible to correct later on.

The instructor demands passive obedience and is careful not to overwork the student. As soon as he feels him tired, he stops. Speed is achieved over time, once the student has perfected all parts of the phrases.

On command: *Engage the sword*, the engagement is made in the sixth or left line;

On command: *Lunge*, the fencer seeks to touch with the tip and raises himself back up.

On command: *On guard*, a pause is taken;

On command: *Gather forward, salute in front of you.*

Article IV

Teaching Progression

1

Flexibility and preparatory movements; sword nomenclature; fingering; salute in arms; coming on guard.

2

Direct line attacks; parries on a change of engagement, on a disengagement, on two disengagements, on one-two, on one-two-three, and the riposte with the straight strike.

3

Varied attacks; high line and low line parries on pressure, *froissement*, beats, *coupé*, *coulé* and the straight strike riposte or compound riposte.

4

Attacks and ripostes while stepping on theme no. 2.

5

Attacks and ripostes while stepping, on theme no. 3.

6

Exercise on the absences of the sword, and how to deceive them.

7

Simple and compound counter-ripostes. Parries of these counter-ripostes.

8

    1. Simple parries with opposition and riposte of the straight strike;

    2. Parries by counter-attack and riposte with the straight strike.

    These parries and ripostes can vary infinitely, depending on the phrases of the instructor or the fencer.

    In sparring,[17] parries, ripostes and counter-ripostes by taking counters are more used, but, on the field,[18] oppositions are better, unless you are very skilled.

Article V

Details of the teaching, flexibility and preparatory movements.

I

The student having successively gone through all the details of the beginning of the teaching - the relaxations and the preparatory movements - the master teaches him the nomenclature of the sword, in order to follow the progression necessary for the study of fencing.

Sword Nomenclature

The buttoned point or weak, with which one touches. Middle, middle part, engagements are made between the middle and the point. Heel, strong part, used for parries.

---

[17] *En assaut*

[18] *sur la terrain*, or, in earnest

Fingering

To my parry of *quarte* or sixth, oppose semicircle *seconde*, sixth, *tierce*, *octave*.

Salute in Arms

1. Bow in front of you.

Put Yourself on Guard

1. On guard (demonstrate and execute).

Stepping

1. Stepping forward or Withdrawing (demonstrate and execute). .

Lunge

1. Extend the arm;

2. Lunge;

3. On guard.

Only touch when the student is in line and in control (demonstrate and have performed).

Gather

1. Gather forward (or backward).

Lines

Left line high on the inside;
Left line low on the inside;
Right line high on the outside;
Right line low on the outside.
Demonstrate and repeat.

Parries

Left line high on the inside, *quarte* and fifth;
Left line low on the inside, *prime* and seventh;
Right line top of outside, sixth and *tierce*;
Right line low on the outside, *seconde* and *octave*.
Demonstrate and repeat.

II

Straight Line Attacks to the Right

At my engagement in sixth or *quarte*,

1. Extend the arm;

2. Lunge;

3. On guard.

By breaking it down or without breaking it down, allowing the touch if the movement is repeated, and parrying if it is changed.

Disengagement

At my disengage:
    Disengage (or oppose and strike straight).

Disengage, Counter, Doublement

At your disengage:

1. I take a counter;

2. Deceive or double;

3. Lunge, touch and return on guard.

Disengage, Counter, Opposition, Deceive, Double and Disengage

At your disengage:

1. I throw a one-two, or one-two-three:

2. Deceive or oppose;

3. Lunge, touch and return on guard.

Disengage, Counter, Opposition, Counter Doubling, Redouble

At your disengage:

1. I take a counter, an opposition and a counter;

2. Deceive, double (or double and redouble);

3. Lunge, touch and return on guard in another line.

Parries

1. After an opposition, parry with an opposition;

2. After a counter, parry with a counter.

Ripostes with the Straight Strike

1. At my engagement in sixth: oppose and strike straight;

2. At my engagement in *quarte*: oppose and strike straight.

1. To my counter of sixth: press the counter and strike straight;

2. To my counter of *quarte*: press the counter and strike straight.

At my engagement:

1. Disengage

2. I oppose;

3. Disengage

4. I oppose;

5. Throw a one-two, or one-two-three:

6. Lunge;

7. On guard.

Deceive the Counter

At your disengage:

1. I take a disengage;

2. Deceive the counter;

3. I take a counter and an opposition;

4. Double and disengage.

One-Two-Three

1. I take two oppositions;

2. Throw a one-two-three;

3. I take two oppositions and one counter;

4. Throw a one-two-three and deceive.

(We throw a one-two-three-four again by taking three oppositions, and, by changing lines, we can also make series of oppositions
and counters.)

III

Pressure, Straight Strike

At my disengage:
1° Press and strike straight;

Beat, Straight Strike

2° Beat, strike straight;

Pressure and Disengagement

3° Press and disengage;

Beat and Disengage

4° Beat and disengage.

Beat or Pressure, One–Two

1° Beat or press, one-two;

Beat or Pressure, One–Two–Three

2° Beat or press, one-two-three;

Beat or Pressure, Double

3° Beat or press, double.

Beat or Pressure, Double, Disengage

4° Beat or press, double, disengage.

Froissement, **Disengage or Strike Straight**

1° *Froissement,* disengage or strike straight;

Froissement, **Doubling**

2° *Froissement,* double;

Froissement, **One–Two**

3° *Froissement,* one-two;

Froissement, **One–Two–Three, Deceive**

4° *Froissement,* one-two-three, deceive.
   At my attacks:

1° Sixth, *quarte* and sixth;   ⎫ Deceive
2° Sixth, *quarte,* counter;   ⎪ the counter,
3° Counter of sixth, counter of *quarte,* sixth; ⎬ oppose,
4 Counter of *quarte,* counter of sixth, *quarte;* ⎪ parry or
                                                  ⎭ riposte

   1. *Coupé,* remain;

   2. *Coupé,* disengage;

   3. *Coulé,* strike straight;

4. *Dérobement*, strike straight.

In the low line,

At my bind: 1° parry by *octave* or seventh, or semicircle;
At my feint: 2° bind and strike above or below;
At my disengage: 3° parry by *octave* or seventh, or semicircle;
At my disengage: 4° take a counter, oppose, parry or riposte.

IV

1° The moves can vary infinitely, between the high line and the low line. You riposte:

By disengaging;
By doubling;
By doing a one-two or one-two-three;
By making a *coupé*;
By opposing;
By taking a counter or two counters.

Attacks are made on a change of engagement, parries after a change of engagement or a riposte.

Attacks are made on a single or double engagement.

Attacks, parries, ripostes, and counter-ripostes are performed while one or both fencers are moving.

V

The Wall and the Assault

This lesson is the application of the aforementioned rules and prepares for the goal of fencing: the assault, preceded by the compound salute, called the wall.

The student will be trained first with a foil then with a combat sword because, for me, fencing with a foil is to the sword what fencing with a wooden sabre is to the regulation sabre, that is to say, the prelude to fencing with the sword and the sabre.

It is undeniable that combined attacks, combined parries, ripostes, and counter-ripostes are always better, as they confuse the opponent more. But, for this, you need a certain amount of strength.

Similarly, fencing in the low line is more advantageous, depending on the strength and size of the fencers. But you must always know how to seize the opponent's strength at the first blow.

Every engagement requires a result, that is, a full on attack without *corps à corps*.

1. Putting oneself on guard must be natural, with perfect balance, shoulders well back, the body upright on the hips. The instructor forces the student to maintain this balance:

2. While stepping;

3. While extending the arm;

4. While lunging (the student will get up quickly to be ready to riposte);

5. While attacking (the student*will start the arm before the foot and will win the engagement*[19]);

6. The counters are intended to unbind the wrist and give speed. They are the best parries for fencers of a certain strength.

The student will attack when he is sure of himself and knows the principles thoroughly. So, he will take care:

1. To stand out of reach, arm half stretched and taking a slight lunge;

2. To break away and move in small steps, always ready to parry;

3. To stretch out one's arm and withdraw preferably to catch one's opponent in his movement;

4. To use simple strikes, and only compound strikes when he does not fear stop strikes;

5. To remember that the counter is the best parry. It brings back or keeps [the sword] in line;

6. To return to guard as soon as the blow is struck;

7. To choose the simplest riposte, after the well finished parry, to avoid the *reprise* or the *remise*;

---

[19] *gagnera sur le fer*

8. To predict the designs of the adversary and to seize his strikes at the right time;

9. To not riposte when the opponent is disarmed;

10. To say: "touched," when his opponent has touched him;

11. To ever speak while fencing and avoid making inappropriate criticism;

12. To leave it to the master and the gallery to judge doubtful blows, and to take a suitable pretext to stop fencing with an unpleasant opponent.

End of Foil Fencing

Part Two – Fencing with the Sabre: or at the *Contre-Pointe*

Fencing schools are schools of observation. It's only through fencing that you can truly understand a man's character.

Article 1

General principles and spirit in which this science must be taught.

The general principles in which sabre fencing should be taught are similar to those of sword.

The master follows the same method and strives to make the *contre-pointe* lesson interesting, which many students do not take seriously enough.

All the qualities essential for a foil fencer are necessary for one who does *contre-pointe*.

Foil fencing is practised in a linear plane, sabre fencing in a linear and circular plane.

Not everyone has the arm and wrist capable of immediately performing the varied plays of the sabre, but with work and perseverance, students always manage to properly handle this formidable weapon, which I would call a true and honest weapon.

Today, sabre fencing is neglected, even in the army: curious anomaly, the cavalrymen only do *pointe*, and not *pointe* and *contre-pointe*! I know very well that, as French people, we prefer thrusts, as they generally yield better results. However, we should not underestimate cuts, which are very effective at incapacitating an opponent!

If the people of the South[20] prefer the sword, those of the North give preference to the sabre. Let us therefore work energetically on both fencing styles, to be able to respond to the needs of war, because I lay down as a principle that if fencing with the sword is essential, that with the sabre is necessary to complete our military education.

Use the sabre as often as possible with thrusts but remember that the sabre is a thrusting and cutting weapon. — Skilfully handled by a strong hand, the sabre is a weapon whose importance cannot be denied.

Of two opponents, one armed with a sabre and the other with a sword, I would certainly wish to be the first. — Miss a disengage, a parry, with the strong of your sword, or a riposte with a straight strike, you are at the mercy of the sabre.

Article II

Description of the sabre, movements and definitions of words used for attack and defence in fencing language.

In the army, we distinguish two models of sabre: that of 1854, for cuirassiers and dragoons, called *latte*, and that of 1822, for chasseurs, hussars, artillerymen, baggage train crews, and called *bancal*.

The first model consists of the blade and the mount. — The blade is straight, with two fullers, with a back, a point, an edge, a heel and a tang engaged in the handle. The mount includes the handle and guard. — The handle or spindle, made of ash or beech, is covered with leather tied with brass wire braid. The guard has three side branches with concave shell.

The second model differs from the first only by a curved blade, called a *bancal*. The guard has only two lateral branches. The other parts are similar to those of the 1854 model.

The weight of the new light cavalry officer's sabre is approximately 680 grams, without the scabbard. The guard is made of nickel-plated steel with three side branches. — This sabre is straight and very easy to hold.

The weight of the exercise sabre, in the fencing halls, is approximately 575 grams. The blade is slightly curved, with a full guard. — This sabre is the assault sabre, because the master generally gives the lesson with wooden sabres (ash or beech).— It is necessary to give real sabres to the students only when they are of a certain strength

---

[20] *du Midi*

with those made of wood. — Before being armed with a real sabre, the student must have a strong wrist and be able to execute a series of feints without tiring, quickly and precisely.

Sabre in the Hand

Take the sabre in the full hand, the thumb extended on the back of the sabre, without touching the guard, the nails underneath, the four fingers together, the hand convex, the thumb used to direct the weapon, the fingers firmly gripping the handle in attacks and parries. The edge is directed to the right, the heel outwards, parallel to the wrist. — The hand should be neither hard nor loose. Depending on the case, it should be firm and soft.

Principal Hand Positions

The two most commonly used positions are:

> *Tierce*, or position on the outside.
> *Quarte*, or position on the inside.

We will return to these positions in the description of the different strikes:

Flexibility[21] or Preparatory Work

As with the sword, the student has to be accustomed to the various flexibility exercises we discussed previously. When he is flexible and agile enough, we move on to movements without a sabre.

Movements Without a Sabre

1. Being in the position of the soldier without weapons, the heels on the same line and close to each other, the feet at right angles, the knees straight, the body plumb on the hips, make a half turn to the left, that is to say a half-quarter circle, pivoting on the left heel and bringing the right foot next to the left foot, keep the head straight, the right arm extended towards the ground, the left forearm joined to the body and bent backwards, the hand resting on the plate, naturally.

---

[21] *les assouplissements*

2. Bend the right arm, the hand at the height of the right breast, the hand closed, the elbow outwards and detached from the body. Bend your thighs and move your right foot 0.60m from your left.

3. Quickly lunge forward with your right leg, your foot perpendicular to your knee. Your left knee should be bent like a spring. Keep your body balanced and moving forward. Extend your right arm straight out in front of you, parallel to the ground. Keep your left arm close to your body, bent backward, with your left hand resting on your hip.

4. Rise to the position of the 2nd movement, bending the left shank, the right foot 0.60m from the left foot, the left forearm joined to the body, the right arm half bent, the hand at breast height.

5. Take position n°1, bringing the right foot next to the left foot, the right arm extended towards the ground.

Stepping

At the position of the 2nd movement, learning to move. — Bring the right foot firmly forward, the body upright, the left foot following at a distance of 0.60 m.

Withdraw

Bring the left foot squarely back, the body still upright, the right foot following at a distance of 0.60m.

The Slip[22] (*Plate 1.*)

To avoid the *contre-pointe* strikes on the leg that one has not parried with the sabre, one escapes with the right leg, bringing it as quickly as possible, always straight, 0.35m behind the left foot, the foot always resting parallel to the ground. — Once the strike has been evaded, return to the guard position (position no. 5).

---

[22]*Échapper*

Guard

Preliminaries to the attack, defence, riposte, and counter-riposte (position for the 2nd movement).

1. In the position of the unarmed soldier, body gathered, sabre in hand, make a half turn to the left, arm extended horizontally.

2. Lower the right arm towards the ground, the tip of the sabre at 0.10m, the left forearm bent backwards, the concave left hand resting on the hip. (*Plate 2.*)

3. Gather the sabre horizontally, the arm still extended. (*Plate 3.*)

4. Raise the sabre, the wrist at shoulder height.

5. Make two *moulinets*: the first to the left, the second to the right. Describe a circle from left to right (or from right to left), passing over the head, letting go of the fingers a little and returning to the position of the hand, the edge to the left or right. Bend your right arm, wrist at right breast height, hand in *tierce* position, nails underneath, elbow slightly out, tip of weapon at eye level with opponent. (*Plate 4.*)

6. Take the position of the 2nd movement, bend the legs and bring the right leg 0.60m from the left foot. (*Plate 5.*)

7. Lunge, extending the right foot after imperceptibly leading with the hand, the left leg supporting the body's weight and acting as a spring, the right knee vertical to the foot, the left forearm always bent and close to the body, the concave hand resting on the hip.

Gathering

Bring the right foot 0.60m from the left, the arm bent, the sabre at the height of the right breast, in the direction of the opponent's eyes. — The gathering is done in front and behind.

Appels

With the body still, strike the ground twice in a row with the right foot. The *appels* are made in the position of the 2nd movement and without preparation.

Échappement de la jambe. (Sabre.)

(Planche 1.)

Slipping the leg. (Sabre) (Plate 1)

Mouvement préparatoire pour se mettre en garde
Première position. (Sabre.)

(Planche 2.)

Preparatory movement to put oneself on guard. First position. (Sabre)
(Plate 2)

Mouvement préparatoire pour se mettre en garde. Deuxième position. (Sabre.)

(Planche 3.)

Preparatory movement to put oneself on guard. Second position. (Sabre) (Plate 3)

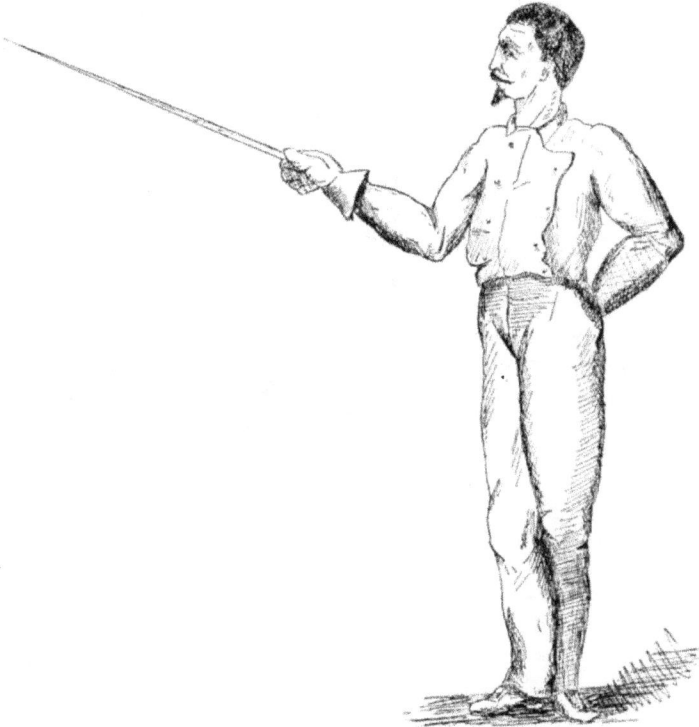

Mouvements préparatoires pour se mettre en garde. Quatrième position. (Sabre.)

(Planche 4)

Preparatory movements to put oneself on guard. Fourth position.
(Sabre) (Plate 4)

Garde. Quatrième position. (Sabre.)

(Planche 5.)

Guard. Fourth position (Sabre.) (Plate 5.)

Stepping Forward

With the body straight, extend the right foot while bringing the left 0.60m from the right.

Stepping Backward

With the body straight, bring the left foot backwards and place the right foot 0.60m from the left foot.

Arm and Wrist Movements. *Moulinets* (*Plate 6.*)

With your arm extended horizontally at the guard position, describe *moulinets* or circular arcs from left to right (or from right to left), finally returning to the guard position. — The wrist plays a big role in the *moulinet*, because it helps the movement. This is a great exercise to loosen up the wrist.

Simple Salute

In the position of an unarmed soldier, that is to say with the body collected, armed with the sabre, go through all the movements of coming on guard, without breaking them down: two moulinets followed by a salute in front of oneself, once collected. — The salute should be made to the right and left in public, then in front of oneself, as prescribed at the end of the compound salute.

Compound Salute or the Wall

Having executed these two *moulinets*, or, in other words, the simple salute, in the on guard position, the compound salute is done:

1. While lunging, deliver a blow to the right;

2. Take the 1st movement of the guard, raising the sabre, the wrist at eye level, the arm extended;

3. Return to guard;

4. Gather forward and cross the sabre;

5. Change guard twice;

6. Withdraw

Moulinet. (Sabre) (Plate 6)

7. Two *appels*;

8. Salute freely to the right and left and gather forward;

9. Return to guard;

10. Precede the attack with these words pronounced by one of the adversaries: *The honour is yours*, let yourself be touched or respond: *In obedience*, while lunging, deliver a flank (or point) blow and return to guard;

11. Salute to the right and to the left, to the right the hand in *tierce*, to the left the hand in *quarte*, then gather behind;

12. Salute in front of yourself.

For this :

1. Carry the sabre in front of the face, arm half extended, hand 0.10 m from the neck, blade vertical, cutting edge to the left, four fingers together, thumb extended on the right side of the handle;

2. Extend your arm, hand in *quarte*, lower the blade towards the ground:

3. To put yourself on guard or withdraw by extending the hand.

Lines

The lines are divided into main lines or lines of engagement, intermediate lines, in which one strikes, and opposition lines, which one uses to cover oneself on the right and left, above and below.

Main Lines

There are two main lines:

Facing the Opponent

1. Right or *tierce* line, or outside zone;

2. Left or *quarte* line, or inside zone.

Intermediate Lines

1. High line, above the wrist;

2. Low line, below the wrist.

The lines of opposition guarantee the blow of the sabre or the point, either by engaging the blade, or by parrying, or by riposting to the left and to the right, above and below, or by counter-riposting.

The wrist joint alone is at play, and while striking the opponent's sabre out of line, one must keep one's own in line, in order to riposte or counter-riposte freely.

In sabre, the hand must be in *tierce* or *quarte*, and not in middle as in sword.

Engagements

To engage the blade is to make contact with the opponent's blade by passing through the shortest line.

To cover oneself is to close the lines.

In both positions, the point of the sabre is at eye level.

Engaging and covering include various variations, depending on the situation.[23]

1. Change of engagement or the counter to the previous engagement;

2. Double engagement or simultaneous engagements.

Fingering

As with the sword, fingering plays a big role in the sabre. The thumb directs the sabre blow, the other four fingers ensure it.

Fingering is a matter of feeling and a gift of nature. A good fencer works hard on his fingering to gain more confidence and precision.

Sabre Strikes

Sabre blows are divided into simple strikes and compound strikes, the first involving only one movement, the others several.

---

[23] *suivant les thèmes*

About the Feeling in Blade[24]

This is pressing the opponent's sabre to make it come out of its line and strike more easily into it to hit it.

Pressing[25]

To press the opposing sabre, press the blade from one end to the other while sliding over it.

Dérobement

This movement is performed by passing the weapon from one line to another and vice versa.

Remise

After the parry, without lifting up, thrust over an absence or abandonment of a sabre.

Reprise

On the parry without riposte, regain contact with the blade without lifting up, and make a touch.

Redoubling

The redoubling consists of two successive attacks.

Stop Strike

In this strike, you have to surprise your opponent in his movement.[26]

Time Strikes

A time strike is a blow that you deal to an opponent who attacks, parries, ripostes or counter-ripostes you too widely.

---

[24] *sentiment dans le fer*
[25] *Écrasement*
[26] *dans sa marche*

Feint

The feint is the beginning of a phrase whose ending is the touch. Feints can be simple or successive. Sabre strikes, between good fencers, generally only have results after a series of feints, to find the opponent's open line.

Parry

The parry is an opposition of the blade. It ends with the touch. Being made with the arm half stretched, you counter-attack more quickly than with the arm bent, as I explain above. Moreover, you avoid the forearm strike.

Sabre Strikes

The sabre strikes are as follows:

Stomach Strike (*Plate 7.*)

Extend your arm and cut the opponent's stomach, using your thumb alone to guide the sabre, hand in *quarte*.

Sash Strike (*Plate 8.*)

Extend your arm and cut off your opponent's shoulder, hand in medium.

Flank Strike (*Plate 9.*)

Extend your arm and cut the opponent's flank, hand in *tierce*.

Forearm Strike

Extend your arm and pass a forearm strike over the opponent's arm, as if to stop the head strike, hand in *tierce* or *quarte*, depending on whether the edge goes to the left or the right.

Face Strike to the Right (*Plate 10.*)

Extend your arm and cut the face to the right. Hand in *tierce*.

Coup de ventre en dedans.
(Planche 7.)

Stomach strike on the inside. (Plate 7)

Coup de banderole.

(Planche 8.)

Sash strike (Plate 8)

Coup de flanc en dehors.
(Planche 9.)

Flank strike on the outside. (Plate 9)

Face Strike to the Left (*Plate 11.*)

Extend your arm and cut the face to the left. Hand in *quarte*.

Thrust[27] (*Plate 12.*)

Extend the arm and deliver a thrust, turning the hand slightly, the edge above and the thumb below, the wrist at head height to parry, if necessary, the head strike with the guard of the sabre. Hand inverted.

Leg Strike[28]

Extend your arm and cut your opponent's leg. Hand in *tierce* or *quarte*, depending on whether the edge goes to the left or right.

Head Strike (*Plate 13.*)

Extend the arm and cut to the head. Hand in middle position.

About the Nine Parries

The parry is an opposition of blade against blade, on the cutting side. Its aim is to drive the opponent's blade from its line. The parry, properly speaking, includes two series.:

1. Body parries, including stomach, sash, flank, forearm, point and leg;

2. Head parries, including head and face, right side and left side.

Stomach Parry

Extend out your right arm and raise it, elbow slightly out, nails forward, forearm parallel to the body, tip of the sabre pointing towards the ground, blade 0.10m from the body, edge turned to the left. — The parry is done in the half-strong of the blade.

Sash Parry

Same parry as for the above, but to execute it, we use the strong of the sabre. — The hand always facing the middle of the body.

---

[27] *Coup de pointe*, or Point Strike
[28] *Coup de jarret*, while literally a hamstring strike, is translated as leg strike.

HAUT

Tête

Figure|Figure

Côté droit   *Côté gauche*

Banderole

Pointe

DEHORS   Manchette   DEDANS

Flanc|Ventre

Jarret

BAS

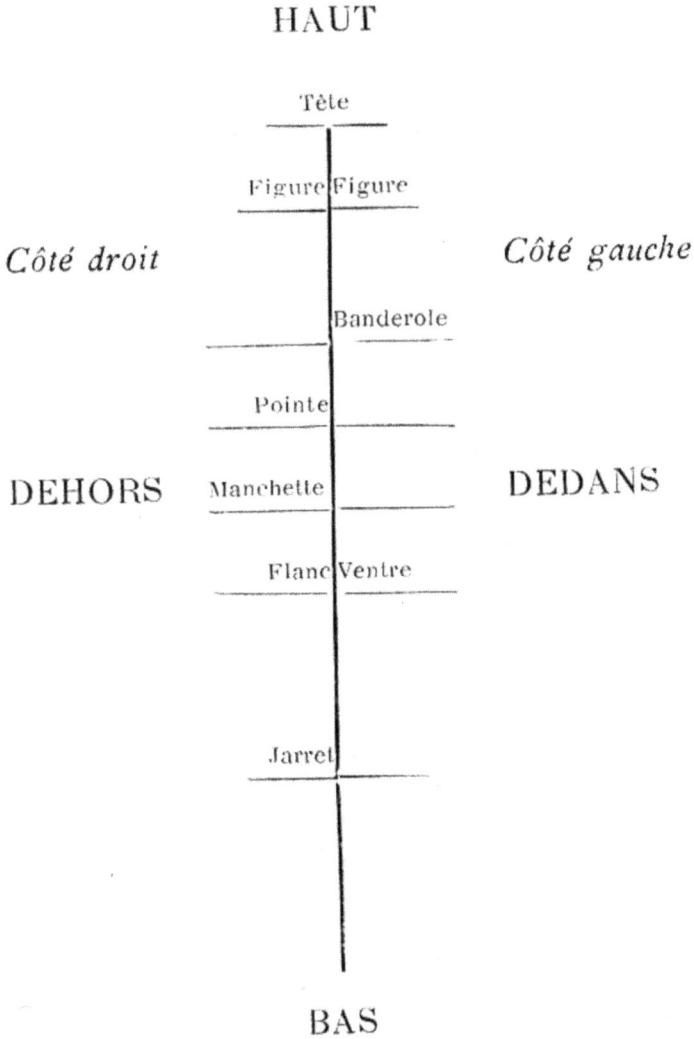

Cutting diagram

Coup de figure en dehors.

(Planche 10.)

Face strike to the outside. (Plate 10)

Coup de figure en dedans (à gauche).

(Planche 11.)

10

Face strike to the inside (left) (Plate 11)

Coup de pointe.
(Planche 12.)

Thrust. (Plate 12)

Coup de tête.
(Planche 13.)

Head strike. (Plate 13)

Flank Parry

Extend the right arm and raise it, the elbow and wrist at shoulder height, as for the stomach parry and the sash parry, the tip of the sabre pointing towards the ground, the blade 0.33 m from the body, the cutting edge to the right. — Parry with half-strong of the blade.

Forearm Parry

Press the blade or parry in *tierce* or *quarte*, depending on the situation.

Thrust Parry

Make an opposition to the opponent's blade, the wrist in the middle of the body.

Leg Parry

Slip the right leg, throwing a head strike. — (Natural riposte.)

Head Parry

Extend and raise the arm, wrist level with the top of the head, blade horizontal, hand turned, nails forward, cutting edge above.

Face Parry on the Right

Extend your arm and place your wrist 0.10m from the breast, the blade a little forward, the cutting edge to the right.

Face Parry on the Left

Extend the arm, place your wrist 0.10m from the breast, the blade a little forward, the cutting edge to the left.

Ripostes and Counter-Ripostes

Do not riposte or counter-riposte except after the completion of a parry and [with] the idea of being able to touch the uncovered side, without uncovering the attacked side.

Stomach Strike

Riposte to the head, sash or flank.

Sash Strike

Riposte to the head, stomach or flank.

Flank Strike

Riposte to the head, sash or stomach.

Forearm Strike

Riposte with a thrust, stomach or flank strike.

Thrust

Riposte to the head, face on the right or face on the left.

Leg Strike

Riposte to the head, stomach or flank.

Head Strike

Riposte with a thrust, stomach or flank strike.

Face Strike to the Right

Riposte with a face strike to the left, flank or stomach strike

Face Strike to the Left

Riposte with a face strike to the right, stomach or flank strike These strikes are executed as counter-ripostes, following the varied play of the situation.

Article III

Statement of the general rules to be observed following the most rational method.

Instruction is given slowly and requires a fair and measured progression to avoid bad principles, always difficult to correct later. The master demands passive obedience, avoiding overworking the student. As soon as he feels him tired, he stops them. — Speed will come with the completion of the phrases and a reasoned reflection.

On command: *On guard*, the engagement is made in *tierce* or *quarte*.

On command: *Lunge*, the fencer tries to deliver a strike to the stomach or flank and lifts himself up on his own.

On command: *On guard*, a pause is taken.

At the command of: *Gather Forward*, salute in front of you.

Article IV

Teaching Progression

I

1. Flexibility and preparatory movements; sabre nomenclature; fingering; salute in arms; coming on guard.

2. Moulinets on the firm foot.

3. Moulinets while lunging

II

1. Simple attacks and simple parries.

2. Simple ripostes and simple counter-ripostes.

3. Summary of these two themes.

III

1. Compound attacks and compound parries.

2. Compound ripostes and compound counter-ripostes.

3. Summary of these two themes.

IV

Varied play, summarising combinations of the above themes.

Article V

Details of the teaching, flexibility and preparatory movements.

I

The student having successively gone through all the details of the beginning of the teaching - the flexibility exercises and the preparatory
movements - the master teaches him the nomenclature of the sabre, in
order to follow the progression necessary for the study of fencing. —
Lessons are given first with a wooden sabre and then with a combat
sabre, when the student is of a certain strength.

Sabre Nomenclature

The weapon composed of a blade and a mount, including the guard.
Point of the sabre or weak, with which one touches. Middle of the
sabre or half-strong, with which one engages the blade. Sabre guard:
strong part; parries are taken a little above this.

Fingering

At my head parry, oppose to the stomach, flank and head.

Salute in Arms

1. Salute in front of you.

Put Yourself on Guard

1. On guard (demonstrate and execute).

Stepping Forward or Withdrawing

1. Stepping forward *or* Withdrawing (demonstrate and execute).

Lunge

1. Extend the arm;

2. Lunge;

3. On guard.

Only touch when the student is in line and in control (demonstrate and have performed).

Gather

1. Gather forward (or backward).

2. Perform the *appels* and salutes.

2nd Moulinets on the firm foot.

The instructor commands:

1° For the moulinets to the right (or left),

1. In position.

2. Begin:

3. Stop.

2° Moulinets to the left (or right).

3° Moulinets to the right and left (or moulinets to the left and right).

3rd. Moulinets while lunging.

1. Moulinets to the right (or left). Lunge.

2. On guard.

3. With a moulinet to the right (or left). Withdraw.

II

1° Simple Attacks and Simple Parries

Attacks
{
Stomach strike;
Sash strike;
Flank strike;
Forearm strike;
Thrust;
Leg strike;
Head strike;
Face strike to the right;
Face strike to the left
}
Lunge. On each strike, the master commands: On guard.

Parries
{
Stomach strike;
Sash strike;
Flank strike;
Forearm strike;
Thrust;
Leg strike;
Head strike;
Face strike to the right;
Face strike to the left
}
Parry. At each parry, the master commands: On guard.

2° Simple ripostes and simple counter-ripostes are executed like the aforementioned attacks.

3° You go through simple attacks, simple parries, simple ripostes and simple counter-ripostes, varying the play with attacks, parries, etc.

III

1° Compound Attacks and Simple Parries

1.
{
1. Feint a stomach strike;
2. On my parry, feint a head strike;
3. On my parry, feint a flank strike.
}

2. $\begin{cases} \text{1. Feint a flank strike;} \\ \text{2. On my parry, feint a head strike;} \\ \text{3. On my parry, flank strike.} \end{cases}$

3. $\begin{cases} \text{1. Feint a sash strike;} \\ \text{2. On my parry, feint a head strike;} \\ \text{3. On my parry, stomach strike.} \end{cases}$

4. $\begin{cases} \text{1. Feint a forearm strike;} \\ \text{2. On my parry, feint a flank strike;} \\ \text{3. On my parry, thrust.} \end{cases}$

5. $\begin{cases} \text{1. Feint a thrust;} \\ \text{2. On my parry, feint a face strike to the right;} \\ \text{3. On my parry, a face strike to the right.} \end{cases}$

6. $\begin{cases} \text{1. Feint a leg strike;} \\ \text{2. On my parry, feint a thrust;} \\ \text{3. On my parry, head strike.} \end{cases}$

7. $\begin{cases} \text{1. Feint a head strike;} \\ \text{2. On my parry, feint a flank strike;} \\ \text{3. On my parry, stomach strike.} \end{cases}$

8. $\begin{cases} \text{1. Feint a face strike to the right;} \\ \text{2. On my parry, feint a face strike to the left;} \\ \text{3. On my parry, flank strike.} \end{cases}$

9. $\begin{cases} \text{1. Feint a face strike to the left;} \\ \text{2. On my parry, feint a face strike to the right;} \\ \text{3. On my parry, stomach strike.} \end{cases}$

With a simple parry, the student must parry the nine blows above.

2° Compound Ripostes and Compound Counter-Ripostes.

Compound ripostes and compound counter-ripostes are successive feints that are executed after the parry.

To parry well, you must regularly follow the opponent's play and not avoid feints which can end in a touch, if the opponent sees the open line.

I will never cease to repeat that good *contre-pointe* fencers parry with their arm almost extended, contrary to the opinion of a great number of masters. In this way, they riposte more quickly and avoid forearm strikes.

IV

Generally, to have a sure result with the sabre, two or three feints are enough to disorient the adversary and allow to have an open line.

With the foil, the simplest moves are often the best. In sabre, compound blows are more successful.

The Wall and the Assault

Every assault is preceded by the exercise called the wall, that is to say, the compound salute.

Fencing bouts with *contre-pointe* are too rare today. Sometimes one sees one, by chance, in fencing meetings with the point. This is a mistake, because the sabre is, par excellence, a combat weapon.

When we bout with *contre-pointe*, we not give too much blade and keep a reasonable distance, not forgetting that with the sabre the blows are made in the direction of the cutting edge, to *cut* or *slice*. Good fingering, a light hand and a quick warning are essential qualities in both *contre-pointe* and pointe fencing. Let us also remember that it is safer to hit by countering than by attacking and, for this, let us parry in good time, with calm, composure, and sure of our strength. Let us be courteous to our adversaries, observe perfect loyalty and banish questions of self-esteem and ridiculous quarrels.

The decor in a fencing hall must be proud and modest to command the respect and esteem of all.

All the efforts of the teacher will tend to instil in the fencers manly feelings and irreproachable conduct under arms.

He will avoid making too lively observations on the fencers' play and will only point out their faults and the means of remedying them during moments of rest.

Finally, driven by the desire to do well and to be useful to their country, teachers and students will hold high the feelings of honour in which the French nation rightly prides itself and will always work towards its defence.

End of the Manual on *Contre-Pointe*.

Study is the love of work. It is the life of the man jealous of preserving his independence.

Fencing Competition Program

1. Reception of civil and military fencing masters;

2. The provosts and student provosts perform group movements;

3. *Contre-pointe* bouts;

4. Great assault of the masters of arms;

5. Assault by civilian and military amateurs;

6. Assault of the provosts and the student provosts;

7. High school students assault;

8. Distribution of prizes.

Ladies will be admitted to attend the competition

Ticket Prices

Firsts : 00 fr.
Seconds : 00 fr.
Third : 00 fr.

Special Provisions

Entrance to the fencing hall is free:

1. For all persons with invitations;

2. For fencers carrying special cards.

General Regulations

Article I

No one will be admitted to compete unless they have registered in advance, in response to the invitation, at the headquarters of the commission and unless they have been included on the list of competitors presented to the jury by the member of the committee delegated for this purpose.

Article II

Formal attire is required.

Article III

Properly equipped changing rooms are available to fencers.

Article IV

The foils used will be numbers 4 and 5. The combat swords are those permitted in fencing halls.

Article V

Silence is required, except for the word *touch*, which is optional to pronounce, under penalty of exclusion.

Article VI

The first assault will last five minutes. The blades will be engaged at the command: "*Begin*", and we will end the assault with a simple salute, at the command: "*Stop.*"

Article VII

The same conditions will be followed in the assaults between the winners of the first round, but they will only last three minutes, as well as the following assaults, until the final classification is reached.

Pointe (Amateurs)

Article I

The jury for the amateur competition will be made up of seven members, composed of:

1. Three fencing masters, drawn by lot;

2. A president and a vice-president drawn by lot and chosen either from among amateurs or from among fencing masters;

3. Two randomly selected amateurs.

Article II

The other arrangements will be those of the fencing masters, with the difference that the first assault will last only three minutes, as will the following ones.

Pointe (Provosts and Student Provosts)

Article I

The jury will be made up of five fencing masters chosen at random.

Article II

The other provisions will be the same as those of the fencing masters.

Pointe (High School Students)

Only Article

Same provisions as for amateurs.

Contre-pointe

The sabres will be made of wood or of the light cavalry model (1824) with shells.

Pointe and *Contre-pointe*

Fencers will use either the left or the right hand. During the assault, hand changes are permitted.

Special Regulations

Pointe (Fencing Masters)

Article I

The fencing masters who present themselves for the assault will draw numbers at random. The pairing of bouts will be between even numbers and odd numbers, following the order.

The opponents will be:

No. 1 with No. 3;
No. 2 with No. 4;

And so on.

Article II

The jury for this competition will be composed as follows:

Each master will draw the name of one of their colleagues, who will serve as their sponsor and who will note, on a pre-printed sheet that they will sign, the hits scored, parries, ripostes, attacks made too high or too low.

Only the admitted strikes will count. In case of a tie, the others will decide.

Article III

These will be null:

1. Strikes with the button that will hit the mask, neck, arm outside the shoulder, or body below the belt;

2. A riposte on a sword strike (for the one who counter-attacked on a hit).

Article IV

1. With full developments, timed [strikes] and stop [strikes] are allowed;

2. A stop [strike] on a disengage on the firm foot which has been touched will be considered good for the attack and not an illegal blow.[29] (Following the principle of parrying first and riposting later);

---

[29] coup fourré

3. The double hit or illegal strike will not count for anyone;

4. In a full riposte, if the sword has left the hand before the riposte, the hit will be null;

5. In the *tac-au-tac* riposte, the strike will be good if it was impossible to predict the disarmament.

Contre-pointe

Article 1

The jury will be formed according to articles I and II of the fencing masters' competition.

Article II

Only the following are permitted:

1. Head strikes and face strikes (*tierce* and *quarte*);

2. The sash (or stomach) strikes;

3. Flank strike

4. Thrusts by development and as stop strikes.

Double hits, called simultaneous hits, do not count for anyone. Note: In the event of a dispute, an honorary jury may be drawn at random.

End of Program

www.ingramcontent.com/pod-product-compliance
Lightning Source LLC
Chambersburg PA
CBHW032006080426
42735CB00007B/518